# CHILD AND HUMAN RIGHTS

**USHA AJITHKUMAR**

*MA [Eng.], MA [HR], MED, PGDHE, Dip. in Journalism*

Assistant Professor,
Hansraj Jivandas College of Education,
Khar, Mumbai.

**First Edition: 2011**

Himalaya Publishing House

MUMBAI • NEW DELHI • NAGPUR • BENGALURU • HYDERABAD • CHENNAI • PUNE • LUCKNOW • AHMEDABAD • ERNAKULAM • BHUBANESWAR • INDORE • KOLKATA

**First Edition : 2011**

**Published by** : Mrs. Meena Pandey for **Himalaya Publishing House Pvt. Ltd.,**
"Ramdoot", Dr. Bhalerao Marg, Girgaon, **Mumbai - 400 004.**
Phone: 2386 01 70/2386 38 63, Fax: 022-2387 71 78
**Email: himpub@vsnl.com Website: www.himpub.com**

**Branch Offices**

**New Delhi** : "Pooja Apartments", 4-B, Murari Lal Street, Ansari Road, Darya Ganj, New Delhi - 110 002. Phone:23270392, 23278631 Fax: 011-23256286

**Nagpur** : Kundanlal Chandak Industrial Estate, Ghat Road, Nagpur - 440 018. Phone: 2738731, 3296733 Telefax: 0712-2721215

**Bengaluru** : No. 16/1 (Old 12/1), 1st Floor, Next to Hotel Highlands, Madhava Nagar, Race Course Road, Bengaluru - 560 001. Phone : 22281541, 22385461, Telefax: 080-22286611

**Hyderabad** : No. 3-4-184, Lingampally, Besides Raghavendra Swamy Matham, Kachiguda, Hyderabad - 500 027. Phone: 040-27560041, 27550139, Mobile: 09848130433

**Chennai** : No. 85/50, Bazullah Road, T. Nagar, Chennai - 600 017. Phone: 044-28144004/28144005

**Pune** : First Floor, "Laksha" Apartment, No. 527, Mehunpura, Shaniwarpeth (Near Prabhat Theatre), Pune - 411 030. Phone: 020-24496323/24496333

**Lucknow** : Jai Baba Bhavan, Church Road, Near Manas Complex and Dr. Awasthi Clinic, Aliganj, Lucknow - 226 024. Phone: 0522-2339329, 4068914, Mobile: 9305302158, 9415349385, 9389593752

**Ahmedabad** : 114, "SHAIL", 1st Floor, Opp. Madhu Sudan House, C.G.Road, Navrang Pura, Ahmedabad - 380 009. Phone: 079-26560126, Mobile: 09327324149, 09314679413

**Ernakulam** : 39/104 A, Lakshmi Apartment, Karikkamuri Cross Rd., Ernakulam, Cochin - 622011, Kerala. Phone: 0484-2378012, 2378016, Mobile: 09344199799

**Bhubaneswar** : 5 Station Square, Bhubaneswar (Orissa) - 751 001. Mobile: 9861046007

**Indore** : Kesardeep Avenue Extension, 73, Narayan Bagh, Flat No. 302, IIIrd Floor, Near Humpty Dumpty School, Narayan Bagh, Indore 452 007(M.P.) Mobile: 09301386468

**Kolkata** : 108/4, Beliaghata Main Road, Near ID Hospital, Opp. SBI Bank, Kolkata - 700 010, Mobile: 09910440956

**Typeset by** : Page Designers, Bengaluru

**Printed by** : Heramb Graphics, Bhandup
Mumbai - 400 078.

*DEDICATED TO*

**THE LOTUS FEET OF**

**MY GURU SHRI SATYA SAI BABA**

**AND**

**MY SON SAISHIVA, MAY GOD BLESS YOU**

# PREFACE

Six years ago, I had no idea how many petals of angst motherhood could unfold. I was simply thrilled about the idea of having a child and joining that special community of women but, self-doubt oozed from underneath every parenting choice I made. I always want my child to live a worthy and dignified life. Eventually, I stumbled onto the subject of child rights and the interest therein motivated me for this book.

This book is for all parents, educators and other stakeholders in education who intend to know about child rights and how to impart it to the students. The main objective of this book is to impart knowledge and skill related to child rights education.

The book is divided into fourteen chapters focusing on Childhood, History of Child Rights, Convention on Child Rights, Child Welfare Activities in India, Education for Child Rights and Child Friendly Schools

It is fitting to close this preface by thanking the many people who made it possible for me to finish this book. My young son Saishiva, who is the inspiration for this book. My brother Shri Krishnan Kutty, my nephew Ashish and neice Vaishnavi need a special mention.

**USHA AJITHKUMAR**

# CONTENTS


| | | |
|---|---|---|
| 1. | CHILDHOOD | 1 - 10 |
| 2. | HISTORY OF CHILD RIGHTS | 11 - 18 |
| 3. | THE UN CONVENTION ON CHILD RIGHTS | 19 - 44 |
| 4. | CHILD ABUSE | 45 - 52 |
| 5. | CHILD WELFARE ACTIVITIES IN INDIA | 53 - 62 |
| 6. | MILESTONES IN CHILD RIGHTS — NATIONAL | 63 - 80 |
| 7. | EDUCATION FOR CHILD RIGHTS —METHODS AND TECHNIQUES | 81 - 88 |
| 8. | EDUCATION FOR CHILD RIGHTS—ACTIVITIES | 89 - 108 |
| 9. | CHILD RIGHTS BASED APPROACH | 109 - 116 |
| 10. | CHILD SURVIVAL | 117 - 124 |
| 11. | CHILD PARTICIPATION —KEY TO EFFECTIVE DEMOCRACY | 125 - 135 |
| 12. | CHILD PROTECTION | 136 - 142 |
| 13. | THE INTEGRATION CHILD PROTECTION SCHEME | 143 - 157 |
| 14. | CHILD FRIENDLY SCHOOLS | 158 - 160 |
| | BIBLIOGRAPHY | 161 - 165 |

# BRIEF CONTENTS

**1. Childhood** **1 - 10**

Introduction — The Significance of Childhood.

**2. History of Child Right** **11- 18**

Introduction —Declaration of Geneva — Declaration of the Rights of the Child —Proclaimed by General Assembly resolution 1386(XIV) of 20 November 1959 with Principles — The Convention on the Rights of the Child, 1989 — The Vienna Declaration — The United Nations Children's Fund — The International Year of the Child — The International Labour Organisation [ILO].

**3. The UN Convention on Child Right** **19- 44**

Introduction — The Four Foundation Principles of the Convention — Convention on Child Rights — Articles — Convention on Child Rights (Child-Friendly Version).

**4. Child Abuse** **45 - 52**

Introduction — Definition of Child Abuse — Physical Indicators of Abuse in the Child — Behavioural Indicators of Abuse in the Child — Parental/familial Indicators in Abusive Families — Child Abuse Across the Globe — Child Abuse in Asia — Child Abuse in India — Study on Child Abuse: India 2007 — Child Survival and Child Health in India — Child Protection — Child Participation.

**5. Child Welfare Activities In India** **53 - 62**

Introduction — Legislations — The National Policy for Children — National Plan of Action for Children 2005 — Schemes/Projects — Integrated Child Development Services (ICDS) Scheme — Integrated Programme for Juvenile Justice — Childline India Foundation (CIF) — Recent Initiatives — The Functions of the Commissions — The Powers of the Commission — Proposed Integrated Programme for Child Services — Other Activities Of Child Welfare — Assistance to Voluntary Organisations for providing Social Defence Services — National Award.

**6. Milestones In Child Rights — National** **63 - 80**

Fundamental Rights — Directive Principles of State Policy — First Five-Year Plan (1951-56) — Second Five-Year Plan (1956-61) — Third Five-Year Plan (1961-66) — Fourth Five-Year Plan (1969-74)— Fifth Five-Year Plan (1974-79) — Sixth Five-Year Plan (1980-85) — The Seventh Five-Year Plan (1985-90) — Eighth Five-Year Plan (1992-97) — Ninth Five-Year Plan (1997-2002) — Tenth Five-Year Plan (2002 – 2007).

**7. Education For Child Rights–Methods And Techniques** **81 - 88**

Introduction — Teaching about and for Human Rights — Teaching and Preaching: Action Speaks Louder than Words — Pedagogical Techniques for Child Rights Education — Factors Affecting Selection Of Strategics — Brainstorming — Case Studies — The Talking Circle Field

Trips/Community Visits — Interviews — Socratic Questioning — Discussion — Visual aids — Research projects — Role-plays/Simulations — Problem Solving — Stories.

**8. Education For Child Rights – Activities** **89 - 108**

Introduction — Appreciating Similarities and Differences — In the Same Boat — Who am I and what am I like? — A Circle for Talking — The Lifeline — Me and My Senses —Wishing Circle —Imaginary Friend — Letters and Friends — Buddy — People around me — The Washing Machine — Blind Trust — Creating Classroom Rules — Classroom Needs — Classroom Responsibilities — Living with Rights and Responsibilities — Understanding Child Rights — Protecting Children — Role-play — Packing your Suitcase — Child Soldiers — Councils and Courts — Words that Wound — Growing Maturity — The Right to Privacy — Discrimination – Stereotypes — The Right to Education — An Adequate Standard of Living — Effects Webs —A Model United Nations (Simulation.)

**9. Child Rights Based Approch** **109 - 116**

Introduction — The UN Convention: Addressing Children's Rights Globally — Adopting a Rights - Based Approach: What does this mean? — Applying a Rights - Based Approach to Programming.

**10 Child Survival** **117 - 124**

Introduction — Under-nutrition cause for Concern — Explaining Under-nutrition What needs to be done?

**11. Child Participation - Key To Effective Democracy** **125 - 135**

Introduction — Definition — Why is Participation Important? — Levels or Ladders of Participation — Ways of Participation — Importance of Child Participation — Key Components of Meaningful Participation of Children — Ethical Issues — Relating to Children Participation.

**12 Child Protection** **136 - 142**

Meaning of Child Protection — Existing Child Protection Mechanism in India — Glaring Gaps in Services.

**13 The Integrated Child Protection Scheme** **143 - 157**

Porpose — Specific Objectives of ICPS — Guiding Principles of ICPS — Approaches of ICPS — ICPS Programme and Activites.

**14. Child Friendly School** **158 - 160**

Introduction — Characteristics of Rights-based, Child Friendly Schools.

**Bibliography** **161 - 165**

**1**

**CHAPTER**

# CHILDHOOD

**"Every child born into this world signifies that God has not lost His trust in Man."—*TAGORE***

Kahlil Gibran in his spiritual work 'The Prophet' presented children as independent beings with autonomous capabilities. He expressed this in the following words:

"Your children are not your children
They are the sons and daughters of Life's longing for itself.
They come through but not from you,
And though they are with you yet they belong not to you.
You may give them your love but not your thoughts,
For they have their own thoughts.
You may house their bodies but not their souls,
For their souls dwell in the house of tomorrow,
Which you cannot visit, not even in your dreams.
You may strive to be like them, but seek not to make them like you.
For life goes not backwards but tarries with yesterday................"

Children are neither mere dolls nor are they lifeless corpses. Happiness is an innate and natural characteristic of children. A society that denies a child its happiness is a lifeless society. A family that gives regard to the happiness of children is one that strives for true joy. All the signs of happiness that a child reflects are in fact its needs for being happy. Children might not have gained the maturity that is expected by elders. They might not have the talent to look at world experiences minutely. But they are not ignorant. Children grow each day. They project this growth every moment. Children do not do wrong things. It is we, who make mistakes in understanding them. It is because of this problem in understanding them that they become a weaker section. It is the society, which refuses to understand the creativity, innocence and sense of equality that is innate in children that bends children according to its cheap values.

Children and childhood across the world, have broadly been construed in terms of a 'golden age' that is synonymous with innocence, freedom, joy, play and the like. It is the time when, spared the rigours of adult life, one hardly shoulders any kind of responsibility or obligations. But, then, it is also true that children are vulnerable, especially when very young. The fact that children are vulnerable, means they need to be cared for and protected from 'the harshness of the world outside' and around. This being so, the adult-child relation, parents in particular, is said to provide 'care and protection' – serving thereby the 'best interests of the child' and meeting their day-to-day 'needs of survival and development'. The adult is presumed to be the guardian and in that respect expected to take the responsibility of child's welfare and development. Whether or not, the premise underlying this is correct or not, the childhood 'reality' on the whole is questionable, demanding critical evaluation. It is indeed a period in a person's life during which she/he is neither expected nor allowed to fully participate in various domains of social life. It is thus, not a world of freedom and opportunity but one of confinement and limitation in which children are 'wholly subservient and dependent'. This being so, childhood is nothing short of a world of isolation, sadness, exploitation, oppression, cruelty and abuse.

Childhood is not a static, objective and universal fact of human nature, but a social construction which is both culturally and historically determined. The history of Hebrews, Greeks and Romans, whose cultures had a great impact upon the Western society, bears testimony to the fact that children, by and large, were taken for granted by their parents and the patriarchal society at large. The resultant effect of all this was that they were treated as objects of intervention rather than as legal subjects in their own right. Many labelled them as a 'problem population' whereas others reduced them to being seen as property and thus, treated them as non-entities. The Roman law, for instance, provided for the *patriae potestas* whereby the father was endowed with absolute power and authority over his family. It included just *vitae necisque*, the power of life and death, and a *fortiori*, of uncontrolled corporal chastisement over wife, children and other family members (Oppenlander, 1981: 386). Ancient Greeks left girls and children born with disabilities on the wild hillsides, where exposure or animals were sure to kill them and the practice was continued routinely in Rome until Christianity became the State religion. The killing of unwanted children may have become less common in the centuries since then, but it never completely disappeared. In the given adult-child power relation, the usual *cliché* of childhood being a 'golden age' not only seemed to be a myth but a distant dream for majority of these children.

The French historian, Philippe Ariès, in his landmark book 'Centuries of Childhood', also claimed that 'the idea of childhood did not exist at all in earlier times', as once the 'child' moved from the biological dependence of 'infancy' it 'belonged to adult society' (Ariès, 1962: 125). According to his analysis, children were 'miniature adults' as they dressed, behaved and conversed similarly, and were engaged in the same social activities and work.

The concept of childhood as a discrete life stage emerged in Europe between the fifteenth and eighteenth centuries as part of a process driven by two primary imperatives. First, there was an affective or *'codlling'* dimension 'in which the child, on account of his, (*sic* ,)sweetness, simplicity and drollery, became a source of amusement and relaxation for the adult'(Ariès, 1962:

126). Second, there was an educational dimension inspired by 'churchmen or gentlemen of the robe ... moralists and pedagogues' (Ariès, 1962: 128-30). This secured control over children's innate 'depravity' and was developed through the influence of the Reformation, with its emphasis on discipline and knowledge of theology, humanities and sciences. It was consolidated during the period of European Enlightenment with the ascendancy of 'rationality'. Initially restricted to the domain of upper-class childhood, Ariès contended that the affective and educational dimensions eventually diffused across society and childhood became institutionalised (Goldson, 1997: 3).

Lloyd de Mause, another historian, in 'The History of Childhood' painted a very negative image of childhood and family life in the past. In fact, he went to the extent of saying that 'the history of childhood is a nightmare from which we have only recently begun to awaken'. He further contended that 'the further back in history one goes, the lower the level of childcare, and the more likely children are to be killed, abandoned, beaten, terrorised and sexually abused' (Mause, 1975: 1-2). According to him, childhood was not discovered in the way that Ariès suggested. On the contrary, it was a human universal that gradually evolved itself from one stage to the other. These stages were:

1. Infanticidal (Antiquity to 4th century A.D.);
2. Abandonment (4th – 13th centuries);
3. Ambivalent (14th – 17th centuries);
4. Intrusive (18th century);
5. Socialisation (19th – mid-20th century);
6. Helping (mid-20th century onwards).

Early Western historians writing about children and their childhood were of the view that till the Middle Ages, abandonment, harsh punishment and the use of fear and other life-inhibiting measures were all part of the era's social history, economics and pattern of families. No doubt, the era of Middle Ages was rightly referred to as the 'Dark Ages'.

Perhaps, an important step in the definition of rights came in 1215, in England. After a period of Civil War, the English nobility forced King John to limit his power, which had been absolute and virtually unchecked, through the *Magna Carta.* Among other things, the *Magna Carta* guaranteed that no free man should be deprived of life, liberty, or property without the due process of law. This in a way provided for the system of *parens patriae* meaning thereby that the sovereign was authorised to act as the 'supreme parent of the child'. The superior 'protective' authority and role of the sovereign provided a basis for interfering with the idea of family privacy and the control of the male head of the household over other members of the family. In other words, the need to protect children's interests gradually began to surface. In a similar development, courts in Roman-Dutch law jurisdiction began to exercise the State's responsibilities as *parens patriae* and came to be considered as the 'upper' or superior guardian of minor children.

At this juncture, it would be worthwhile to pause and look at the overall status of children in India, especially with regard to the overall treatment meted out to them by their parents and the society at large. Historically, we all know that the major caretaker of a child was the mother, the immediate family or, at best, the joint family and secondarily jati (caste) relationships. Sudhir Kakar, who has made a detailed analysis of Indian childhood and society in his book *'The Inner World — A Psycho-Analytic Study of Childhood and Society in India'* has dwelled at length on mother-child relationship and how this profoundly influences the 'quality' and 'dynamics' of social relations throughout one's life (Kakar, 1982:52-112). Consistent with the belief that life begins with conception rather than at birth, five stages of childhood were identified in the Indian tradition. These were: (i) Garbha, or the foetal period; (ii) Ksheerda (0-6 months), when the infant lives entirely on milk; (iii) Ksheerannada (6 months-2 years), the period of early childhood in which weaning takes place; (iv) Bala (2-5 years); and (v) Kumara (5-16 years). Each of these divisions of childhood were associated with major rites and rituals, which marked its transition from one period to another.

Many of these childhood samskaras — like namakarana (naming ceremony), mundan (tonsure ceremony) and upanayana (initiation into religion and wider community) are being performed even today with fanfare by the people of India. These samskaras, in a way, emphasised the critical period both in biological as well as social development thus, paving the way for the gradual integration of the child into society. Ironically, girls and children belonging to the lower castes were largely excluded from these samskaras (Kakar, 1981: 204-07). For instance, the sohras – joyous songs of celebration sung at the birth of a child in the Hindi speaking belt – are almost never sung for newborn daughters. In fact, many sohras express the relief of mother's over the fact that she has been blessed with a son and not a daughter (Kakar, 1981: 207). The preference for a son when a child is born, thus, seems to be as old as the Indian society itself.

Our two great epics, the Ramayana and the Mahabharata also eulogise the Indian view of childhood whereby there is an intense parental longing for children, and their upbringing is characterised by affectionate indulgence. This 'child centeredness', however, was found to be limited to boys only. The Indian tradition all along has been indifferent, if not overtly hostile, to the developmental fate of girls. Secondly, the Indian tradition subscribed to an ideology that downgraded the role of the environment and nurture in the development of a child, and instead emphasised upon a deterministic conception of mystical heredity. This mystical heredity in the Mahabharata was reduced to the karmas of the previous life and the attributes of the father (especially his caste) transmitted through his 'seed' (Kakar, 1981: 199-200). These epics also displayed as to how young children, especially boys, were placed under the tutorship and guidance of respected gurus, wherein moral precepts enjoined in the shastras were taught on a one-to-one basis. But, this too, was confined to the boys of the ruling upper-castes. Likewise, in ancient Indian law, especially in the Laws of Manu, the child though located very near the bottom of a social pyramid was bestowed society's protection. And, this protective indulgence was best reflected in matters which concerned the children most – namely, their chastisement. Children were only to be beaten with a rope or bamboo stick split at the end. The split bamboo, as we may remember from circus clowns' mock fights, makes a loud noise but does not inflict much pain. Moreover, even this punishment was to be carried out only on the back and never on the head or the chest. All those who hold progressive views on child discipline, the beating of children may hardly seem like 'protective indulgence'. Nonetheless, the extent of this indulgence becomes strikingly clear when we compare Manu's Laws with legal texts of other ancient societies where brutal forms of child abuse and maltreatment existed. As already mentioned in the beginning, there is evidence in the law codes and digests of ancient Rome to suggest that brutal forms of child abuse were common mistreatment, which the more enlightened emperors attempted to mitigate. And, that it was only as late as 374 A.D. that infanticide was declared a capital offence in the Roman world. In short, though Manu's Laws by modern standards have been severely condemned as a repository of inequity, their attitude towards children – one of protective nurturance– is unexceptionable, at least within the premises of the patriarchal society which gave the Laws their birth. Surprisingly, Manu also expressed that kindness be shown to the daughter as she is 'physically more tender and her emotions are more delicate'.

Interestingly, though historical and sociological documentation of early Indian civilisation points out towards the pervasive biases of that time in the upbringing of children, on account of factors like caste, kinship, age, gender and the like. Rulers like Ashoka (268-31 B.C.), Chandragupta Vikramaditya (c. A.D. 375-415) tried to propound moral edicts as a counter-balance in which obedience towards parents and respect for elders was extolled. In nutshell, the point driven home was that loyalty and obedience to one's elders, was not only moral but also socially approved and valued behaviour.

For an account of children and childhood in the Indian literary tradition, let us also take a look at the classical Sanskrit literature. Here, the child curiously seems to have appeared as a wish — that is, in the context of a couple's, or more often a father's, longing for offspring — or as the fulfilment of the wish — in descriptions of parental happiness when a child was born and in lyrical accounts of parental love, usually of a father for his son. On the whole, children rarely figured as individuals in their own right, with activities, reactions and feelings separate from those of their all-powerful parents. Bhavabhuti's description of Rama's love for Lava and Kusha, and Banbhatta's rhapsodization over Prabhakarvardhan's love for his son, Harsha, are two well-known examples that could be cited here. Kalidasa, the greatest of all Sanskrit poets, too was lyrical in his descriptions about the father's feeling for his son, but at the same time he sensitively portrayed, with much empathy, the sage Kanva's love for his daughter Shakuntala. Needless to mention, the classics of the regional languages are also replete with rich accounts of children and childhood. It would be useful to mention here the medieval Hindi literature associated with the Bhakti movement, especially the songs of Surdasa on Krishna's childhood and that of Tulsidasa on Rama's childhood. The verses of these songs, till date, are a rich source for Hindu ideals of childhood and for delineating the topography of a culturally approved utopia of childhood. Besides, the Bhakti poetry laid enormous emphasis on the loving relationship between mother and child. Analogous to the mother child interplay, or rather as its extension, we find a third theme in Bhakti literature in which the child is at the centre of an admiring circle of adults. If the mother is in the foreground, then the background consists of the adults in the community– the gopis of Gokul, the citizens of Ayodhya – milling around him. This particular theme reveals the child's primary need to be central to his world, rather than exist forlornly at its outskirts, to cause a glow in the eyes of adults rather than be looked at with indifference (Kakar, 1981: 200-204).

In traditional India, thus, in comparison to the West, it was early childhood rather than adulthood that was considered to be the 'golden age' in individual's life history. Shashi Pande has distinguished Western and Indian social relations by suggesting that in the West, intimacy in a relationship develops out of some shared activity, as when a father takes his son on hunting and fishing trips as a means of developing (or proving) a mutual trust and camaraderie, whereas no such 'hidden agenda' is needed for a cultivation of a relationship in Indian society (Pande, 1968: 425-32). However, before getting lost in any self congratulatory adulation, we must also note that the gravest drawback of the Indian tradition was the inferior status accorded to girl children. For girls, in comparison to boys, learning the mandatory skills of household work, cooking and childcare, etc. constituted the daily activities around which their lives revolved. In this, of course, the mother, grandmother, aunts, sisters and sisters-in-laws, her allies against the discriminations and inequities of the existent patriarchal order and values groomed her. In fact, late childhood marked the beginning of an Indian girl's deliberate training in how to be a 'good woman', and hence, the conscious inculcation of culturally designated feminine roles. M.N. Srinivas, in his book, *Marriage and Family in Mysore,* writes that "It is the mother's duty to train her daughter up, to be an absolute docile daughter-in-law…' (Srinivas, 1942: 195). Girls were also married at an early age, which invariably marked the end of their childhood. The low status accorded to the girl child was perhaps one of the reasons for the prevalence of female infanticide in traditional India which continues to exist even today.

With the coming of the Arabs, Turks, Afghans and the Mughals, the medieval period stretching across from the eleventh to seventeenth centuries almost, saw an all-round impoverishment and degeneration in India. The foreign invasions not only plundered but completely destroyed the wealth and sociocultural ethos of India. Due to the overall economic deterioration experienced by the people, the children too faced adverse vicissitudes. Imposition of foreign culture had a profound impact at all levels. Families, and particularly those of the preponderant rural population, could no longer afford wholesome food and amenities for their children. Emphasis on elementary education gradually withered away which was quite widespread earlier. Among the Hindus, elementary education was mostly confined to the higher castes like Brahmins, Rajputs and Vaishyas. Elementary education among the Muslims was given to those who belonged to aristocratic and rich families at home through the Maulvis. Others had to go to the maktabs situated in mosques. Girls, on the other hand, were seldom given education and their status in comparison to boys remained inferior. The rulers or the people took no remedial steps either.

During this period, in India too, the early legal statements were conspicuously silent on children's rights. The Ten Commandments, arguably the most influential of all legal codes, contains a clear normative pronouncement on parent-child relations but it is in terms of respect for parents and is silent on the obligation of parents to love and nurture children. One of the earliest recognitions of children's rights perhaps are found in the Massachusetts Body of Liberties of 1641 where parents are told not to choose their children's mates and not to use unnatural severity against their children. Children, furthermore, were given 'free liberty to complain to the Authorities for redress'. But this was also the law that prescribed the death penalty for children over 16 who disobeyed parents. There is no evidence though that children did successfully litigate against their parents but nor is there any that disobedient children were executed. The document, nevertheless, remains interesting in showing, as it does, that even some 365 years ago protection of children went hand in hand with adding the power of the State to parental authority (Freeman, 1997: 47-48).

The eighteenth century as well can hardly be said to be identified with children's rights. It is pertinent to remark that the documents emanating from the great libertarian revolutions, the American and the French, have nothing specifically to say about children (Freeman, 1997:48).

The nineteenth century, however, saw the birth of the child-saving movement, the growth of the orphanage, the development of child protection legislations, schooling and the construction of separate institutions, including the juvenile courts, for delinquent children, in different parts of the Western world. One of the reasons for this kind of development was that in the wake of Industrial Revolution there was severe exploitation of many working-class children who were widely employed in textiles, mining, agriculture, domestic service, docks and navigation. Moreover, the so-called 'advances' of industrialization and urbanization had serious consequences. Displacement of communities, unemployment and socio-political unrest resulted in marginalization and abandonment of many children whose 'opportunities' were restricted to petty offending as means of survival. These children were left to their fate to fend for themselves. At this point of time, the British ruled India. Being a colony of the British, the plight of its children especially those belonging to the lower strata of society was certainly gloomy. As Britain was negotiating its place within a new emerging economic, social and political world order, it was a time of great uncertainty for India and this inevitably affected its children too. Despite all this, moral panic and political reaction of that time dovetailed into the already existing reform and philanthropic efforts towards children which mobilised charity crusades and inspired voluntary effort. But, all this took a back seat in the face of growing imperialism of that time that had taken one of its worst forms. This development spelled doom for children as they were thought of as 'Bricks for Empire Building' and like others continued to be exploited in different ways. The ensuing freedom struggle, that nearly spread over 100 years – from mid-nineteenth to the mid-twentieth century – aimed not merely at achieving political independence from the British rule, but also at reinvigorating the debilitated sunken society of India which under decades of slavery had lost its initiative, values and vitality.

It was the endeavour of leaders like Raja Ram Mohan Ray, Mahatma Gandhi and others to awaken the people and rouse them to overcome their backwardness, be it in the shape of illiteracy or socio-cultural practices like child marriage or neglect in the upbringing of children, etc. As a result, the long years of struggle for freedom saw an all-round spate of activities which may be termed as 'social action' so to come out of the prevailing weaknesses in society and to build self reliance in the people. Consequently, the care of the child came to be viewed upon as a vital element in the resurrection of the nation. Mahatma Gandhi and later Pt. Jawaharlal Nehru, in person, gave much of their time to inculcate social concern for the citizens of tomorrow – the children. Advancing literacy, in Western societies, to a large extent, helped to change attitudes towards children. The resultant effect of all this was that a large number of dedicated visionaries, charitable and voluntary organisations moved by the harrowing tales of children, worked relentlessly to improve the overall position of children in society along with that of women. All of them invested their time, knowledge and resources towards better health, education, and growth of the weaker children. It was during this period that some of the oldest voluntary organizations such as 'The Children's Aid Society' and 'Balkan Ji Bari' came into being in 1920s in the service of children belonging to the poor, uneducated and helpless families. The entire century of freedom struggle may well be termed as the Evanescent Dawn of Voluntary Action when people learnt to pool their common resources to remove social ills rather than rely upon an alien regime which had no State Policy nor a programme to meet the needs of children. This was also the beginning of a spirit of independence at the group social action level (Luthra, 1979: 90-91). This period also witnessed the enactment of laws such as the Apprentices Act, Reformatory Schools Act and Factories Act which became important factors in the shaping and structuring of a new childhood.

The period immediately following the First World War, posed a variety of challenges to Britain and other countries of Europe and North America. These were mainly connected to the question of how they could create a society which would preclude the cataclysm of violence and upheaval through which they had just passed. It would be worthwhile to mention that partly as a result of the ravages of war on the civilians in affected countries, and partly in response to the growing concern in most countries of Europe and North America for the protection of children, the newly formed League of Nations established a Committee on Child Welfare in 1919 (Lundy, 1997: 21).

Interestingly, private agencies felt the need to provide broad social standards for the protection of children. Of particular importance was the Save the Children International Union, inspired largely by the work of an English woman, Eglantyne Jebb, who had founded Save the Children in response to her own experience with child victims of war in the Balkans. In 1923, the Save the Children International Union adopted as its charter a five-point declaration which described the basic conditions a society should meet in order to provide adequate protection and care for its children. The next year, the Union persuaded the League of Nations to adopt the same declaration.

Since the League of Nations held its meetings in Geneva, this 1924 Declaration of the Rights of the Child came to be known as the "Declaration of Geneva".

Recognising that 'mankind owes to the child the best that it has to give', the five simple principles of the Declaration established the basis of child rights in terms of both protection of the weak and vulnerable and promotion of the child's development. The Declaration also made it clear that the care and protection of children was no longer the exclusive responsibility of families or communities or even individual countries; the world as a whole had a legitimate interest in the welfare of all children.

The League of Nations, as we all know, was not able to prevent another world war. The Second World War engulfed the entire planet, and caused even greater suffering for non-combatants, particularly children. In 1945, the United Nations Organisation replaced the League of Nations. In 1946, the Economic and Social Council of the United Nations recommended that the Geneva Declaration be reaffirmed as a sign of commitment to the cause of children. The same year, the United Nations established a specialised agency — UNICEF with a mandate to care for the world's children. Initially known as the United Nations International Children's Emergency Fund, it provided assistance to children in Europe and elsewhere who had lost homes, family, and opportunity as a result of the war. Its mandate was later redefined so as to give the agency responsibility for long-term assistance to children who suffered from deprivation caused by economic and political conditions, as well as the effects of war. The present nomenclature of UNICEF is United Nations Children's Fund.

We all know that there is no universal picture of children or for that matter childhood. Moreover, for understanding childhood it is important to demystify the glory of any one class, caste, region, gender or time. The need of the hour is to unpack the manner in which children and childhood so far have been understood. Rights are entitlements; they are trumps; they are valuable commodities. And they are also, as we now learn weapons to undermine power. A rights strategy is one way in which the hitherto excluded can be included, within the community and within the socio-economic and political structure.

## THE SIGNIFICANCE OF CHILDHOOD

What was childhood for? Two broad theoretical positions have emerged on this question. One argues that childhood is a characteristic of human evolution designed to ensure the survival and development of the species. The other suggests that the state of childhood or how childhood is viewed is significant in itself as an indicator of the evolution or development of societies and cultures toward notions of civility or modernity. The former, which encompasses the *biosocial* and *evolutionary* approaches, argues that childhood, as a stage of growth and development, has evolved in human society to provide the conditions for optimizing the prospects of maturity. In particular, this perspective has suggested that the distinctively rapid growth of the brain and the immaturity of dentition and digestive tracts characteristic of the early stages of human life have evolved over time to sustain human society. Such a view is consistent with an essentialist or universal view of childhood (that prioritizes biology over environment in explaining childhood) but has also recognized that social conditions and ecology play a part in constructing the social and cultural response to childhood. Somewhat related to bio-social theories, the perspective of evolutionary psychology came to regard childhood as directly linked to the evolution of what has been called a psychology of *Parenting*. This theory suggests that certain universal characteristics of infants and young children, such as relatively large heads and eyes in small bodies, act to trigger instinctive emotions and responses in adults, thus securing development toward maturity.

From this perspective, childhood can be seen as a relationship and therefore can be understood in generational terms. The principle relationship of childhood is with adulthood, but more specifically with parenthood. The development or evolution of conscious parenting is the focus of a school of thought known as *psychohistory,* which has developed since the 1970s following the work of Lloyd De Mause. De Mause and his associates have developed a distinctive and controversial theory of childhood. This position establishes from empirical evidence that childhood, while seemingly held by society to be a time of freedom and innocence, has been for the majority of children a time of oppression and abuse. De Mause has argued that the parental response to the infant or child has evolved over time from one which was generally abusive and cruel to one which became nurturing and affectionate. Such a development, according to this theory, not only reflected social, technological, and cultural change but indeed generated those changes.

For *Sigmund Freud* (1856–1939) and psychotherapists who have followed Freud, such as Alice Miller, childhood was of key significance in the adjustment of the individual to mature well-being. Freud developed his theories of the sub-conscious partly through considering the reasons early childhood memory becomes lost. Since childhood was regarded as the key stage in the successful, or unsuccessful, development of ego, psychological well-being in adult life hinged on this period of time and healing might be effected through the recall of repressed childhood experience.

☆☆☆☆☆

# 2 CHAPTER HISTORY OF CHILD RIGHTS

**"There is no trust more sacred than the one the world *holds* with children. There is no duty more important than ensuring that their rights are respected, that their welfare is protected, that their lives are free from fear and want and that they can grow up in peace."** — ***Kofi Annan***

According to international law, a 'child' means every human being below the age of 18 years. Childhood is a process through which every human being passes. Children are more vulnerable than adults to the conditions under which they live. The world's culture and future hang on the practical concern shown for the worth and growth of the child, its environments and opportunities. Children take over from the elders, the responsibilities of maintaining, developing and transmitting civilisation and all facets of the creative development of human personality and of unfolding the cultural richness, social, ethical and aesthetic values which bring out the full potentialities and dimensions of human life. There has been a universal concern for the welfare and protection of the rights of the child for quite some time past. It began as early as 1924 with a landmark declaration on the 'Rights of Child'.

**1923/24:**

Recognition of Children as individuals with inalienable Rights, began under International Law in 1924, when the League of Nations adopted in Geneva, a Declaration on Children's Right, abolishing the custom of treating children as the property of their father. It was thus, in the beginning of the 20th century, that a new meaning was developed that children were essential Human Resources whose mature form would determine future of society.

**1959 :**

UN Declaration on the Rights of the Child

**1989:**

UN Convention on the Rights of the Child

**1990:**

The UN Commission on the Human Rights appoints a Special Rapporteur on the Sale of Children, Child Prostitution and Child Pornography.

**1990:**

World Summit for Children in New York. Adoption of a World Declaration and Plan of Action for the Survival, Protection and Development of Children.

**1990:**

African Charter on the Rights and Welfare of the Child

**1996:**

Graca Machal submits her groundbreaking study "Impact of Armed Conflict on Children" to the UN – General Assembly

**1998:**

Six international NGOs form the Coalition to Stop the Use of Child Soldiers in order to lobby for a ban on the use of children in war and armed conflict

**1999:**

The Human Security Network develops out of a group of like-minded countries, with a strong emphasis on the situation of children affected by armed conflict

**1999:**

Convention No. 182 on the Worst Forms of Child Labor Organisation adopted by the International Labor Organisations

**2000:**

Adoption of two Optional Protocols to the Convention on the Involvement of Children in Armed Conflict and the Sale of Children, Child Prostitution and Child Pornography

**2002:**

The UN Commission on Human Rights mandates a major study on violence towards children

**2002:**

Children's Forum and UN General Assembly Special Session on Children in New York Declaration and Plan of Action adopted.

## DECLARATION OF GENEVA

Since the League of Nations held its meetings in Geneva, the 1924 Declaration of the Rights of the Child came to be known as the "Declaration of Geneva".

Recognising that 'mankind owes to the child the best that it has to give', the five simple principles of the Declaration established the basis of child rights in terms of both protection of the weak and vulnerable and promotion of the child's development. The Declaration also made it clear that the care and protection of children was no longer the exclusive responsibility of families or communities or even individual countries; the world as a whole had a legitimate interest in the welfare of all children.

The gist of the "Declaration of Geneva" is given below-

- Child must be given the means needed for its normal development, both material and non material
- Hungry child should be fed; sick child should be helped; erring child should be reclaimed; and the orphan and the homeless child should be sheltered and succoured.
- Child must be first to receive relief in times of distress.
- Child must be put in a position to earn a livelihood and must be protected against every form of exploitation.
- Child must be brought up in the consciousness that its best qualities are to be used in the service of its fellow men.

In 1948, the United Nations General Assembly adopted the Universal Declaration of Human Rights (UDHR). The UDHR contains three specific references about children and their rights. Article 25 states that "motherhood and childhood are entitled to special care and assistance", and adds that "All children, whether born in or out of wedlock, shall enjoy the same social protection". In Article 26, which deals with the right to education, provision is made to ensure that "Parents have a prior right to choose the kind of education that shall be given to their children". Thus, when the UDHR was adopted, it was assumed that children's rights had been taken care of on the whole. But, this was, however, not found to be fully adequate to the situation of children in the post-Second World War era.

Recognising that Childhood and Youth are subject to many visible and invisible sufferings and disabilities and exploitations, the International Covenant on Economic, Social and Cultural Rights provide that "Special measure of protection and assistance should be taken on behalf of all children and young persons without any discrimination for reasons of parentage or other conditions.

Children and young persons should be protected from economic and social exploitation. Their employment in work harmful to their morals or health or dangerous to life or likely to hamper their normal development should be punishable by law. States should also set age limits below which the paid employment of child labour should be prohibited by law". {Art. 10[3]}.

The State parties to the International Covenant on Cultural and Political Rights also recognizes the need that "Every child shall have without any discrimination as to race, colour, sex, language, religion, national or social origin, property or birth – the right to such measures of protection as are required by his status as a minor, on the part of his family, society or state. {Art. 24 [1]}

Children were recognised as a particularly vulnerable group, who needed specific measures directed towards their protection and the provision of rights that would permit their full and healthy development. It was in this background that the General Assembly adopted the Declaration of the Rights of the Child. The 1959 Declaration expanded the five principles of the Geneva Declaration to ten basic principles.

## DECLARATION OF THE RIGHTS OF THE CHILD

Later, in furtherance of the Geneva Declaration on Rights of Child, the General Assembly of the United Nations Organisations, with the representatives of 78 countries, unanimously adopted 'The Declaration of the Rights of the Child' on 20th of November, 1959. It consisted of 10 principles which enriched and developed the 1924 Geneva Declaration.

### Proclaimed by General Assembly resolution 1386(XIV) of 20 November 1959

*Whereas* the peoples of the United Nations have, in the Charter, reaffirmed their faith in fundamental human rights and in the dignity and worth of the human person, and have determined to promote social progress and better standards of life in larger freedom, *Whereas* the United Nations has, in the Universal Declaration of Human Rights, proclaimed that everyone is entitled to all the rights and freedoms set forth therein, without distinction of any kind, such as race, colour, sex, language, religion, political or other opinion, national or social origin, property, birth or other status, *Whereas* the child, by reason of his physical and mental immaturity, needs special safeguards and care, including appropriate legal protection, before as well as after birth, *Whereas* the need for such special safeguards has been stated in the Geneva Declaration of the Rights of the Child of 1924, and recognized in the Universal Declaration of Human Rights and in the statutes of specialized agencies and international organizations concerned with the welfare of children, *Whereas* mankind owes to the child the best it has to give, *Now therefore, The General Assembly Proclaims* this Declaration of the Rights of the Child to the end that he may have a happy childhood and enjoy for his own good and for the good of society the rights and freedom herein set forth, and calls upon parents, upon men and women as individuals, and upon voluntary organizations, local authorities and national Governments to recognize these rights and strive for their observance by legislative and other measures progressively taken in accordance with the following principles:

**Principle 1**

The child shall enjoy all the rights set forth in this Declaration. Every child, without any exception whatsoever, shall be entitled to these rights, without distinction or discrimination on account of race, colour, sex, language, religion, political or other opinion, national or social origin, property, birth or other status, whether of himself or of his family.

**Principle 2**

The child shall enjoy special protection, and shall be given opportunities and facilities, by law and by other means, to enable him to develop physically, mentally, morally, spiritually and socially in a healthy and normal manner and in conditions of freedom and dignity. In the enactment of laws for this purpose, the best interests of the child shall be the paramount consideration.

**Principle 3**

The child shall be entitled from his birth to a name and a nationality.

**Principle 4**

The child shall enjoy the benefits of social security. He shall be entitled to grow and develop in health; to this end, special care and protection shall be provided both to him and to his mother, including adequate pre-natal and post-natal care. The child shall have the right to adequate nutrition, housing, recreation and medical services.

**Principle 5**

The child who is physically, mentally or socially handicapped shall be given the special treatment, education and care required by his particular condition.

**Principle 6**

The child, for the full and harmonious development of his personality, needs love and understanding. He shall, wherever possible, grow up in the care and under the responsibility of his parents, and, in any case, in an atmosphere of affection and of moral and material security; a child of tender years shall not, save in exceptional circumstances, be separated from his mother. Society and the public authorities shall have the duty to extend particular care to children without a family and to those without adequate means of support. Payment of State and other assistance towards the maintenance of children of large families is desirable.

**Principle 7**

The child is entitled to receive education, which shall be free and compulsory, at least in the elementary stages. He shall be given an education which will promote his general culture and enable him, on a basis of equal opportunity, to develop his abilities, his individual judgement, and his sense of moral and social responsibility, and to become a useful member of society.

The best interests of the child shall be the guiding principle of those responsible for his education and guidance; that responsibility lies in the first place with his parents.

The child shall have full opportunity for play and recreation, which should be directed to the same purposes as education; society and the public authorities shall endeavour to promote the enjoyment of this right.

**Principle 8**

The child shall in all circumstances be among the first to receive protection and relief.

**Principle 9**

The child shall be protected against all forms of neglect, cruelty and exploitation. He shall not be the subject of traffic, in any form.

The child shall not be admitted to employment before an appropriate minimum age; he shall in no case be caused or permitted to engage in any occupation or employment which would prejudice his health or education, or interfere with his physical, mental or moral development.

**Principle 10**

The child shall be protected from practices which may foster racial, religious and any other form of discrimination. He shall be brought up in a spirit of understanding, tolerance, friendship among people, peace and universal brotherhood, and in full consciousness that his energy and talents should be devoted to the service of his fellow men.

Like its predecessor, the 1959 Declaration was no more than a statement of good intentions. For, there was no way to bind the Member States of the United Nations in order to put the principles of the Declaration into practice. Besides, the Declaration looked at children purely as an investment. It did not accord any recognition to their autonomy or for that matter to the importance of their wishes and feelings, nor any appreciation to their empowerment. The child only remained as an object of concern, rather than a person with self-determination.

## THE CONVENTION ON THE RIGHTS OF THE CHILD, 1989

Exactly after 30 years, i.e., on 20th of November, 1989 the General Assembly of the United Nations adopted unanimously the 'Convention on the Rights of Child' which is a complete document on the rights of child. It was ratified by 107 member States within a year and India was one of the signatories to it. The significance of this convention lies in the fact that it has revolutionized the concept of the rights of child by introducing two elements in it. First, it has widened the perspective of the right of the child not by treating him as a mere beneficiary of special protection and assistance but rather as an active person possessing certain rights. Secondly for the effective implementation of the rights contained therein, the convention lays down certain measures such as obligation of the state, parties to the convention to respect and ensure the rights set forth in the convention to each child within it's jurisdiction, their obligation to provide information to both adults and children regarding the rights of the child and their obligation to publicize their reports on the implementation of rights of the child. [This Convention is discussed in detail in the next chapter]

## THE VIENNA DECLARATION

The Vienna Declaration and Programme of Action, which was adopted by the United Nations World Conference on Human Rights on 25th June, 1993, with a spiritual touch and moral reach, makes a humanist summons on nations, in the articles relating to the rights of child. The World Conference on Human Rights reiterates the principles of "First Call for Children" and in this respect, underlines the importance of major national and international efforts, especially, those of the United Nations Children's Fund {UNICEF}, for promoting respect for the rights of the child to survival, protection, development and participation. It demands that measures should be taken to achieve universal ratification of the Convention on the Rights of the Child, by 1995.

It calls on the States to integrate the Convention on the Rights of Child into their National Action Plan, with the support of international cooperation to address the acute problem of children under especially difficult circumstances. Exploitation and abuse of children should be actively combated, including by addressing their root causes.

## THE UNITED NATIONS CHILDREN'S FUND

The General Assembly established the "United Nations International Children's Emergency Fund'", UNICEF, on 11th of December, 1946 to provide assistance to children and adolescents of those countries which had been the victims of aggression. Later, it was decided that the Fund would continue to provide assistance to the children in the developing countries and in those countries which had been devastated by war or other calamities. The name has been changed to 'United Nations Children's Fund' but the acronym, 'UNICEF' has been retained

## THE INTERNATIONAL YEAR OF THE CHILD

The International Year of the Child was observed in the year 1979 as the 20th anniversary of the adoption of the 1959 Declaration of the Rights of the Child, marked by activities at regional, national and international levels, under the essential leadership of UNICEF, for the protection and promotion of the rights of the child which was followed by the 'International Decade of the Child'.

## THE INTERNATIONAL LABOUR ORGANISATION [ILO]

The ILO is the UN's specialized agency which seeks the promotion of social justice and internationally recognized human and labour rights. It was founded in 1919 and formulates international labour standards in the form of conventions and recommendations, setting minimum standards of basic labour rights. In 1919, its first year of inception, the ILO adopted Convention No. 5 on the minimum age for the industrial sector. Since then it remained a major international forum for addressing Child Labour issues. The other irrelevant ILO Conventions are,

1. Convention No. 29 - Forced labour 1930
2. Convention No. 59 - Minimum Age for Industrial Sector [Revised] 1937
3. Convention No. 105 – Abolition of Forced Labour, 1957
4. Convention No. 123 – Minimum Age for Underground Work 1965
5. Convention No. 138 – Minimum Age for Admission to Employment 1973

The ILO Convention No. 138 serves as the principal standard on child labour. This was passed in 1973 and signed by over 60 countries. The signatories are required to set a minimum work age standard of 15 years, although exemptions are included which permit countries whose economy and educational facilities are insufficiently developed to initially specify a minimum age of 14 years.

☆☆☆☆☆

3

CHAPTER

# THE UN CONVENTION ON CHILD RIGHTS

**"If I have brightened up one single sad childhood, then I have at least accomplished something in my life."** ***—Astrid Lindgren***

The UN Convention on the Rights of the Child is the most comprehensive human rights document ever adopted by the international community. Forty-two countries spent 10 years drafting the *Convention*. All but two countries in the world —the United States and Somalia — have ratified it. Built on varied legal systems and cultural traditions, the *Convention* is a universally agreed set of non-negotiable standards and obligations linking the child and fundamental human rights. Notably, the *Convention* is the first legally binding international instrument to incorporate the full range of human rights — civil, political, economic, social and cultural, and it is the most comprehensive treaty for the protection and support of children in existence today. The *Convention* is also the only international human rights treaty that gives NGOs an explicit role in monitoring its implementation.

The CRC is "the most complete statement of child rights ever made." It takes the ten principles of the 1959 Declaration of the Rights of the Child, and expands them to 54 articles, of which 41 relate specifically to the rights of children, covering almost every aspect of a child's life. It is indeed an innovative document in overall human rights theory and practice. In fact, it is the first United Nations human rights instrument since the UDHR which brings together as inextricable elements of the life of an individual human being the full range of civil and political rights, and economic, social and cultural rights. It can do this because it treats children as complete individuals, rather than as elements in an economic or socio-political system. The Convention aims to create a balance between the rights of children and those of the parents or adults responsible for their survival, development and protection. This is achieved by according children the right to participate in decisions concerning them and their future. It is, thus, a holistic document for each article is intertwined with the others. Not only this, the various articles exert an influence on the interpretation and implementation of each other. In other words, the rights defined in the Convention are interdependent as none of the articles can be dealt in isolation. They have to be applied and implemented simultaneously if at all the rights of every child is to be respected.

The CRC had behind it the full resources of UNICEF which, having decided that the Convention was in the best interest of the child, determined to achieve the target of universal ratification as a top priority. Allied with UNICEF in this effort was a worldwide network of non-governmental organisations, focussed in the NGO Group on the Convention. These included Save the Children Alliance, which had a long standing claim of priority in the field of child rights, and Defence for Children International, which chaired the NGO Ad-hoc Group that worked on the negotiation of the Convention. Many of the proposals made by the NGO Ad-hoc Group for the Convention were adopted by the Government representatives on the Working Group, and are reflected in the final text of the Convention. The resultant effect of all this was that in virtually every country there was a coherent and concerted pressure for ratification applied by UNICEF from the outside, and by national non-governmental coalitions or coordinating committees for child rights from the inside. The net outcome was that by, 2nd September 1990, just over 8 months after the Convention had been opened for signature, the twentieth ratification had been received and the Convention came into effect – more quickly than any other human rights treaty. The previous record for this kind was held by the Convention on the Elimination of All Forms of Discrimination Against Women (CEDAW), which also had a strong non-governmental lobby pushing for its ratification in many countries, but it took almost three times as long as the CRC to come into effect.

When a country ratifies a UN Convention, it becomes law within its territory. To monitor progress achieved in the realisation of children's rights, the CRC has established an international expert body, the Committee on the Rights of the Child, which provides awareness and understanding of the principles and provisions of this treaty. The CRC Committee consists of ten experts which ensures that the law is being enforced. The Government of India ratified the CRC on 11th December 1992. As of now, except for Somalia and the United States of America, all the countries around the world have ratified the CRC.

The Convention not only provides for monitoring of the performance of States Parties at the international level but also what is being done for children at the national level. Article 43 sets out the criteria for the establishment of the United Nations Committee on the Rights of the Child, which receives and reviews reports prepared by States, Parties about their progress in implementing the Convention as required by Article 44. Unlike other international initiatives that have been taken on behalf of children, in particular, the Declaration and Plan of Action that emerged out of the World Summit for Children that was held at New York in September 1990, there is no requirement *per se* that the Convention is to be fully implemented by all countries within a stipulated date. Instead, all countries are required to make constant progress towards its implementation, but at a rate that suits their economic and political situation within the resources that are available to them. In a nutshell, the CRC does not have a time limit nor does it have an expiry date. The obligations on countries to live up to the rights of children will not cease, but will continue to require action and attention of each one of us, including the Government, to take the onus of protecting and respecting rights of children not because of an international agreement but because "that's just the way children are to be treated." A Special Rapporteur has also been appointed on the Sale of Children, Child Prostitution and Child Pornography by the United Nations General Assembly who analyses instances of sexual exploitation of children in various countries.

The Convention legally guarantees all children:

- The right to survival.
- The right to develop to the fullest.
- The right to protection from harmful influences, abuse and exploitation.
- The right to participate fully in family, cultural and social life

## THE FOUR FOUNDATION PRINCIPLES OF THE CONVENTION

Among the 54 Articles that make up the *Convention*, four have been identified as the 'foundation' principles that serve as a guide to interpreting all other articles:

### Article 2: Non-Discrimination

The principle of non-discrimination (on the basis of race, colour, sex, language, opinion, origin, disability, religion, birth or any other characteristic) means that all children have the same right to develop to their potential.

### Article 3: Best Interests of the Child

The best interests of the child is to be 'a primary consideration' in all actions regarding children. This principle is key because:

a. It supports a child-centred approach; focusing attention on the child's inter-related rights and needs, rather than on one particular need or programmatic response.

b. It provides a basis for evaluating the laws, policies and practices of States Parties with regard to the protection provided to children.

c. It makes the case that basic services for children must be protected at all times, including during periods of economic reforms and deficit reduction.

### Article 6: Right to Life, Survival and Development

This principle recognizes that in all countries there are children living in exceptionally difficult conditions, and that such children need special consideration. Among other things, this principle is based on the concept of 'distributive justice', which implies the adoption of positive measures to ensure that policies truly cover and reach all children. In this regard, it is crucial to take into account the issue of accessibility, which seeks to guarantee the right to basic services and equity of opportunity for all individuals to achieve their full development.

### Article 12: The Right to Participation

This article highlights children's right to participate in decisions that affect their lives, and to have their views duly considered, according to their age and maturity. Participation is frequently defined as: "... the process of sharing decisions which affect one's life and the life of the community in which one lives. It is the means by which democracy is built and it is a standard against which democracies should be measured." 20th November is celebrated as the international day for children. The United Nations General Assembly recommended in 1954 (Resolution 836 (IX)) that all countries institute a Universal Children's Day, to be observed as a day of understanding between children and of activity promoting the welfare of the world's children. The date of 20th November marks the day on which the Assembly adopted the Declaration of the Rights of the Child, in 1959, and the Convention on the Rights of the Child, in 1989.

## CONVENTION ON CHILD RIGHTS

### Preamble

The States Parties to the present Convention, Considering that, in accordance with the principles proclaimed in the Charter of the United Nations, recognition of the inherent dignity and of the equal and inalienable rights of all members of the human family is the foundation of freedom, justice and peace in the world.

Bearing in mind that the peoples of the United Nations have, in the Charter, reaffirmed their faith in fundamental human rights and in the dignity and worth of the human person and have determined to promote social progress and better standards of life in larger freedom.

Recognizing that the United Nations has, in the Universal Declaration of Human Rights and in the International Covenants on Human Rights, proclaimed and agreed that everyone is entitled to all the rights and freedoms set forth therein, without distinction of any kind, such as race, colour, sex, language, religion, political or other opinion, national or social origin, property, birth or other status.

Recalling that, in the Universal Declaration of Human Rights, the United Nations has proclaimed that childhood is entitled to special care and assistance.

Convinced that the family, as the fundamental group of society and the natural environment for the growth and well-being of all its members and particularly children, should be afforded the necessary protection and assistance so that it can fully assume its responsibilities within the community.

Recognizing that the child, for the full and harmonious development of his or her personality, should grow up in a family environment, in an atmosphere of happiness, love and understanding,

Considering that the child should be fully prepared to live an individual life in society and brought up in the spirit of the ideals proclaimed in the Charter of the United Nations and in particular in the spirit of peace, dignity, tolerance, freedom, equality and solidarity.

*Bearing in mind* that the need to extend particular care to the child has been stated in the Geneva Declaration of the Rights of the Child of 1924 and in the Declaration of the Rights of the Child adopted by the General Assembly on 20th November 1959 and recognized in the Universal Declaration of Human Rights, in the International Covenant on Civil and Political Rights (in particular in articles 23 and 24), in the International Covenant on Economic, Social and Cultural Rights (in particular in article 10) and in the statutes and relevant instruments of specialized agencies and international organizations concerned with the welfare of children.

*Bearing in mind* that, as indicated in the Declaration of the Rights of the Child, "the child, by reason of his physical and mental immaturity, needs special safeguards and care, including appropriate legal protection, before as well as after birth,".

*Recalling* the provisions of the Declaration on Social and Legal Principles relating to the Protection and Welfare of Children, with Special Reference to Foster Placement and Adoption Nationally and Internationally; the United Nations Standard Minimum Rules for the Administration of Juvenile Justice (The Beijing Rules); and the Declaration on the Protection of Women and Children in Emergency and Armed Conflict,

*Recognizing* that, in all countries in the world, there are children living in exceptionally difficult conditions and that such children need special consideration.

*Taking due account* of the importance of the traditions and cultural values of each people for the protection and harmonious development of the child.

*Recognizing* the importance of international co-operation for improving the living conditions of children in every country, in particular in the developing countries. Have agreed as follows:

## Part I

### Article 1

For the purpose of the present Convention, a child means every human being below the age of eighteen years unless under the law applicable to the child, majority is attained earlier.

### Article 2

1. States Parties shall respect and ensure the rights set forth in the present Convention to each child within their jurisdiction without discrimination of any kind, irrespective of the child's or his or her parent's or legal guardian's race, colour, sex, language, religion, political or other opinion, national, ethnic or social origin, property, disability, birth or other status.
2. States Parties shall take all appropriate measures to ensure that the child is protected against all forms of discrimination or punishment on the basis of the status, activities, expressed opinions, or beliefs of the child's parents, legal guardians, or family members.

### Article 3

1. In all actions concerning children, whether undertaken by public or private social welfare institutions, courts of law, administrative authorities or legislative bodies, the best interests of the child shall be a primary consideration.

2. States Parties undertake to ensure the child such protection and care as is necessary for his or her well-being, taking into account the rights and duties of his or her parents, legal guardians, or other individuals legally responsible for him or her, and, to this end, shall take all appropriate legislative and administrative measures.
3. States Parties shall ensure that the institutions, services and facilities responsible for the care or protection of children shall conform with the standards established by competent authorities, particularly in the areas of safety, health, in the number and suitability of their staff, as well as competent supervision.

**Article 4**

States Parties shall undertake all appropriate legislative, administrative and other measures for the implementation of the rights recognized in the present Convention. With regard to economic, social and cultural rights, States Parties shall undertake such measures to the maximum extent of their available resources and, where needed, within the framework of international co-operation.

**Article 5**

States Parties shall respect the responsibilities, rights and duties of parents or, where applicable, the members of the extended family or community as provided for by local custom, legal guardians or other persons legally responsible for the child, to provide, in a manner consistent with the evolving capacities of the child, appropriate direction and guidance in the exercise by the child of the rights recognized in the present Convention.

**Article 6**

1. States Parties recognize that every child has the inherent right to life.
2. States Parties shall ensure to the maximum extent possible the survival and development of the child.

**Article 7**

1. The child shall be registered immediately after birth and shall have the right from birth to a name, the right to acquire a nationality and, as far as possible, the right to know and be cared for by his or her parents.
2. States Parties shall ensure the implementation of these rights in accordance with their national law and their obligations under the relevant international instruments in this field, in particular where the child would otherwise be stateless.

**Article 8**

1. States Parties undertake to respect the right of the child to preserve his or her identity, including nationality, name and family relations as recognized by law without unlawful interference.

2. Where a child is illegally deprived of some or all of the elements of his or her identity, States Parties shall provide appropriate assistance and protection, with a view to re-establishing speedily his or her identity.

**Article 9**

1. States Parties shall ensure that a child shall not be separated from his or her parents against their will, except when competent authorities subject to judicial review determine, in accordance with applicable law and procedures, that such separation is necessary for the best interests of the child. Such determination may be necessary in a particular case such as one involving abuse or neglect of the child by the parents, or one where the parents are living separately and a decision must be made as to the child's place of residence.
2. In any proceedings pursuant to paragraph 1 of the present article, all interested parties shall be given an opportunity to participate in the proceedings and make their views known.
3. States Parties shall respect the right of the child who is separated from one or both parents to maintain personal relations and direct contact with both parents on a regular basis, except if it is contrary to the child's best interests.
4. Where such separation results from any action initiated by a State, Party, such as the detention, imprisonment, exile, deportation or death (including death arising from any cause while the person is in the custody of the State) of one or both parents or of the child, that State Party shall, upon request, provide the parents, the child or, if appropriate, another member of the family with the essential information concerning the whereabouts of the absent member(s) of the family unless the provision of the information would be detrimental to the well-being of the child. States, Parties shall further ensure that, the submission of such a request shall of itself entail no adverse consequences for the person(s) concerned. . . .

**Article 10**

1. In accordance with the obligation of States Parties under article 9, paragraph 1, applications by a child or his or her parents to enter or leave a State Party for the purpose of family reunification shall be dealt with by States, Parties in a positive, humane and expeditious manner. States, Parties shall further ensure that the submission of such a request shall entail no adverse consequences for the applicants and for the members of their family.
2. A child whose parents reside in different States shall have the right to maintain on a regular basis, save in exceptional circumstances personal relations and direct contacts with both parents. Towards that end and in accordance with the obligation of States Parties under article 9, paragraph 1, States, Parties shall respect the right of the child and his or her parents to leave any country, including their own, and to enter their own country. The right to leave any country shall be subject only to such restrictions as are prescribed by law and which are necessary to protect the national security, public order, public health or morals or the rights and freedoms of others and are consistent with the other rights recognized in the present Convention.

**Article 11**

1. States Parties shall take measures to combat the illicit transfer and non-return of children abroad.

2. To this end, States, Parties shall promote the conclusion of bilateral or multilateral agreements or accession to existing agreements.

**Article 12**

1. States Parties shall assure to the child who is capable of forming his or her own views the right to express those views freely in all matters affecting the child, the views of the child being given due weight in accordance with the age and maturity of the child.

2. For this purpose, the child shall in particular be provided the opportunity to be heard in any judicial and administrative proceedings affecting the child, either directly, or through a representative or an appropriate body, in a manner consistent with the procedural rules of national law.

**Article 13**

1. The child shall have the right to freedom of expression; this right shall include freedom to seek, receive and impart information and ideas of all kinds, regardless of frontiers, either orally, in writing or in print, in the form of art, or through any other media of the child's choice.

2. The exercise of this right may be subject to certain restrictions, but these shall only be such as are provided by law and are necessary:

    a. For respect of the rights or reputations of others; or

    b. For the protection of national security or of public order (order public), or of public health or morals.

**Article 14**

1. States Parties shall respect the right of the child to freedom of thought, conscience and religion.

2. States Parties shall respect the rights and duties of the parents and, when applicable, legal guardians, to provide direction to the child in the exercise of his or her right in a manner consistent with the evolving capacities of the child.

3. Freedom to manifest one's religion or beliefs may be subject only to such limitations as are prescribed by law and are necessary to protect public safety, order, health or morals, or the fundamental rights and freedoms of others.

**Article 15**

1. States Parties recognize the rights of the child to freedom of association and to freedom of peaceful assembly.

2. No restrictions may be placed on the exercise of these rights other than those imposed in conformity with the law and which are necessary in a democratic society in the interests of national security or public safety, public order, the protection of public health or morals or the protection of the rights and freedoms of others.

**Article 16**

1. No child shall be subjected to arbitrary or unlawful interference with his or her privacy, family, home or correspondence, nor to unlawful attacks on his or her honour and reputation.
2. The child has the right to the protection of the law against such interference or attacks.

**Article 17**

States Parties recognize the important function performed by the mass media and shall ensure that the child has access to information and material from a diversity of national and international sources, especially those aimed at the promotion of his or her social, spiritual and moral well-being and physical and mental health. To this end, States Parties shall:

1. Encourage the mass media to disseminate information and material of social and cultural benefit to the child and in accordance with the spirit of article 29;
2. Encourage international co-operation in the production, exchange and dissemination of such information and material from a diversity of cultural, national and international sources;
3. Encourage the production and dissemination of children's books;
4. Encourage the mass media to have particular regard to the linguistic needs of the child who belongs to a minority group or who is indigenous;
5. Encourage the development of appropriate guidelines for the protection of the child from information and material injurious to his or her well-being, bearing in mind the provisions of articles 13 and 18.

**Article 18**

1. States Parties shall use their best efforts to ensure recognition of the principle that both parents have common responsibilities for the upbringing and development of the child. Parents or, as the case may be, legal guardians, have the primary responsibility for the upbringing and development of the child. The best interests of the child will be their basic concern.
2. For the purpose of guaranteeing and promoting the rights set forth in the present Convention, States Parties shall render appropriate assistance to parents and legal guardians in the performance of their child-rearing responsibilities and shall ensure the development of institutions, facilities and services for the care of children.
3. States Parties shall take all appropriate measures to ensure that children of working parents have the right to benefit from child-care services and facilities for which they are eligible.

**Article 19**

1. States Parties shall take all appropriate legislative, administrative, social and educational measures to protect the child from all forms of physical or mental violence, injury or abuse, neglect or negligent treatment, maltreatment or exploitation, including sexual abuse, while in the care of parent(s), legal guardian(s) or any other person who has the care of the child.

2. Such protective measures should, as appropriate, include effective procedures for the establishment of social programmes to provide necessary support for the child and for those who have the care of the child, as well as for other forms of prevention and for identification, reporting, referral, investigation, treatment and follow-up of instances of child maltreatment described heretofore, and, as appropriate, for judicial involvement.

**Article 20**

1. A child temporarily or permanently deprived of his or her family environment, or in whose own best interests cannot be allowed to remain in that environment, shall be entitled to special protection and assistance provided by the State.

2. States Parties shall in accordance with their national laws ensure alternative care for such a child.

3. Such care could include, *inter alia,* foster placement, kafalah of Islamic law, adoption or if necessary placement in suitable institutions for the care of children. When considering solutions, due regard shall be paid to the desirability of continuity in a child's upbringing and to the child's ethnic, religious, cultural and linguistic background.

**Article 21**

States Parties that recognize and/or permit the system of adoption shall ensure that the best interests of the child shall be the paramount consideration and they shall:

1. Ensure that the adoption of a child is authorized only by competent authorities who determine, in accordance with applicable law and procedures and on the basis of all pertinent and reliable information, that the adoption is permissible in view of the child's status concerning parents, relatives and legal guardians and that, if required, the persons concerned have given their informed consent to the adoption on the basis of such counselling as may be necessary;

2. Recognize that inter-country adoption may be considered as an alternative means of child's care, if the child cannot be placed in a foster or an adoptive family or cannot in any suitable manner be cared for in the child's country of origin; (c) Ensure that the concerned child by inter-country adoption enjoys safeguards and standards equivalent to those existing in the case of national adoption;

3. Take all appropriate measures to ensure that, in inter-country adoption, the placement does not result in improper financial gain for those involved in it;

5. Promote, where appropriate, the objectives of the present article by concluding bilateral or multilateral arrangements or agreements, and endeavour, within this framework, to ensure that the placement of the child in another country is carried out by competent authorities or organs.

**Article 22**

1. States Parties shall take appropriate measures to ensure that a child who is seeking refugee status or who is considered a refugee in accordance with applicable international or domestic law and procedures shall, whether unaccompanied or accompanied by his or her parents or by any other person, receive appropriate protection and humanitarian assistance in the enjoyment of applicable rights set forth in the present Convention and in other international human rights or humanitarian instruments to which the said States are Parties.

2. For this purpose, States Parties shall provide, as they consider appropriate, co-operation in any efforts by the United Nations and other competent intergovernmental organizations or non-governmental organizations co-operating with the United Nations to protect and assist such a child and to trace the parents or other members of the family of any refugee child in order to obtain information necessary for reunification with his or her family. In cases where no parents or other members of the family can be found, the child shall be accorded the same protection as any other child permanently or temporarily deprived of his or her family environment for any reason, as set forth in the present Convention.

**Article 23**

1. States Parties recognize that a mentally or physically disabled child should enjoy a full and decent life, in conditions which ensure dignity, promote self-reliance and facilitate the child's active participation in the community.

2. States Parties recognize the right of the disabled child to special care and shall encourage and ensure the extension, subject to available resources, to the eligible child and those responsible for his or her care, of assistance for which application is made and which is appropriate to the child's condition and to the circumstances of the parents or others caring for the child. Recognizing the special needs of a disabled child, assistance extended in accordance with paragraph 2 of the present article shall be provided free of charge, whenever possible, taking into account the financial resources of the parents or others caring for the child, and shall be designed to ensure that the disabled child has effective access to and receives education, training, health care services, rehabilitation services, preparation for employment and recreation opportunities in a manner conducive to the child's achieving the fullest possible social integration and individual development, including his or her cultural and spiritual development

3. States Parties shall promote, in the spirit of international cooperation, the exchange of appropriate information in the field of preventive health care and of medical, psychological and functional treatment of disabled children, including dissemination of and access to information concerning methods of rehabilitation, education and vocational services, with the aim of enabling States Parties to improve their capabilities and skills and to widen their experience in these areas. In this regard, particular account shall be taken of the needs of developing countries.

**Article 24**

1. States Parties recognize the right of the child to the enjoyment of the highest attainable standard of health and to facilities for the treatment of illness and rehabilitation of health. States, Parties

shall strive to ensure that no child is deprived of his or her right of access to such healthcare services.

2. States Parties shall pursue full implementation of this right and, in particular, shall take appropriate measures:

   a. To diminish infant and child mortality;

   b. To ensure the provision of necessary medical assistance and healthcare to all children with emphasis on the development of primary healthsscare;

   c. To combat disease and malnutrition, including within the framework of primary health care, through, *inter alia,* the application of readily available technology and through the provision of adequate nutritious foods and clean drinking-water, taking into consideration the dangers and risks of environmental pollution;

   d. To ensure appropriate pre-natal and post-natal health care for mothers;

   e. To ensure that all segments of society, in particular parents and children, are informed, have access to education and are supported in the use of basic knowledge of child health and nutrition, the advantages of breastfeeding, hygiene and environmental sanitation and the prevention of accidents;

   f. To develop preventive health care, guidance for parents and family planning education and services.

3. States Parties shall take all effective and appropriate measures with a view to abolishing traditional practices prejudicial to the health of children.

4. States Parties undertake to promote and encourage international co-operation with a view to achieving progressively the full realization of the right recognized in the present article. In this regard, particular account shall be taken of the needs of developing countries.

**Article 25**

States Parties recognize the right of a child who has been placed by the competent authorities for the purposes of care, protection or treatment of his or her physical or mental health, to a periodic review of the treatment provided to the child and all other circumstances relevant to his or her placement.

**Article 26**

1. States Parties shall recognize for every child the right to benefit from social security, including social insurance, and shall take the necessary measures to achieve the full realization of this right in accordance with their national law.

2. The benefits should, where appropriate, be granted, taking into account the resources and the circumstances of the child and persons having responsibility for the maintenance of the child, as well as any other consideration relevant to an application for benefits made by or on behalf of the child.

**Article 27**

1. States Parties recognize the right of every child to a standard of living adequate for the child's physical, mental, spiritual, moral and social development.

2. The parent(s) or others responsible for the child have the primary responsibility to secure, within their abilities and financial capacities, the conditions of living necessary for the child's development.

3. States Parties, in accordance with national conditions and within their means, shall take appropriate measures to assist parents and others responsible for the child to implement this right and shall in case of need provide material assistance and support programmes, particularly with regard to nutrition, clothing and housing.

4. States Parties shall take all appropriate measures to secure the recovery of maintenance for the child from the parents or other persons having financial responsibility for the child, both within the State Party and from abroad. In particular, where the person having financial responsibility for the child lives in a State different from that of the child, States Parties shall promote the accession to international agreements or the conclusion of such agreements, as well as the making of other appropriate arrangements.

**Article 28**

1. States Parties recognize the right of the child to education, and with a view to achieving this right progressively and on the basis of equal opportunity, they shall, in particular:

   a. Make primary education compulsory and available free to all;

   b. Encourage the development of different forms of secondary education, including general and vocational education, make them available and accessible to every child, and take appropriate measures such as the introduction of free education and offering financial assistance in case of need;

   c. Make higher education accessible to all on the basis of capacity by every appropriate means;

   d. Make educational and vocational information and guidance available and accessible to all children;

   e. Take measures to encourage regular attendance at schools and the reduction of drop-out rates.

2. States Parties shall take all appropriate measures to ensure that school discipline is administered in a manner consistent with the child's human dignity and in conformity with the present Convention.

3. States Parties shall promote and encourage international cooperation in matters relating to education, in particular with a view to contributing to the elimination of ignorance and illiteracy throughout the world and facilitating access to scientific and technical knowledge and modern teaching methods. In this regard, particular account shall be taken of the needs of developing countries.

**Article 29**

1. States Parties agree that the education of the child shall be directed to:

   a. The development of the child's personality, talents and mental and physical abilities to their fullest potential;

   b. The development of respect for human rights and fundamental freedoms, and for the principles enshrined in the Charter of the United Nations;

   c. The development of respect for the child's parents, his or her own cultural identity, language and values, for the national values of the country in which the child is living, the country from which he or she may originate, and for civilizations different from his or her own;

   d. The preparation of the child for responsible life in a free society, in the spirit of understanding, peace, tolerance, equality of sexes, and friendship among all peoples, ethnic, national and religious groups and persons of indigenous origin;

   e. The development of respect for the natural environment.

2. No part of the present article or article 28 shall be construed so as to interfere with the liberty of individuals and bodies to establish and direct educational institutions, subject always to the observance of the principle set forth in paragraph 1 of the present article and to the requirements that the education given in such institutions shall conform to such minimum standards as may be laid down by the State.

**Article 30**

In those States in which ethnic, religious or linguistic minorities or persons of indigenous origin exist, a child belonging to such a minority or who is indigenous shall not be denied the right, in community with other members of his or her group, to enjoy his or her own culture, to profess and practise his or her own religion, or to use his or her own language.

**Article 31**

1. States Parties recognize the right of the child to rest and leisure, to engage in play and recreational activities appropriate to the age of the child and to participate freely in cultural life and the arts.

2. States, Parties shall respect and promote the right of the child to participate fully in cultural and artistic life and shall encourage the provision of appropriate and equal opportunities for cultural, artistic, recreational and leisure activity.

**Article 32**

1. States Parties recognize the right of the child to be protected from economic exploitation and from performing any work that is likely to be hazardous or to interfere with the child's education, or to be harmful to the child's health or physical, mental, spiritual, moral or social development.

2. States Parties shall take legislative, administrative, social and educational measures to ensure the implementation of the present article. To this end, and having regard to the relevant provisions of other international instruments, States Parties shall in particular:

   a. Provide for a minimum age or minimum ages for admission to employment;

   b. Provide for appropriate regulation of the hours and conditions of employment;

   c. Provide for appropriate penalties or other sanctions to ensure the effective enforcement of the present article.

**Article 33**

States Parties shall take all appropriate measures, including legislative, administrative, social and educational measures, to protect children from the illicit use of narcotic drugs and psychotropic substances as defined in the relevant international treaties, and to prevent the use of children in the illicit production and trafficking of such substances.

**Article 34**

States Parties undertake to protect the child from all forms of sexual exploitation and sexual abuse. For these purposes, States Parties shall in particular take all appropriate national, bilateral and multilateral measures to prevent:

(a) The inducement or coercion of a child to engage in any unlawful sexual activity;

(b) The exploitative use of children in prostitution or other unlawful sexual practices;

(c) The exploitative use of children in pornographic performances and materials.

**Article 35**

States Parties shall take all appropriate national, bilateral and multilateral measures to prevent the abduction of, the sale of or traffic in children for any purpose or in any form.

**Article 36**

States Parties shall protect the child against all other forms of exploitation prejudicial to any aspects of the child's welfare.

**Article 37**

States Parties shall ensure that:

a. No child shall be subjected to torture or other cruel, inhuman or degrading treatment or punishment. Neither capital punishment nor life imprisonment without possibility of release shall be imposed for offences committed by persons below eighteen years of age;

b. No child shall be deprived of his or her liberty unlawfully or arbitrarily. The arrest, detention or imprisonment of a child shall be in conformity with the law and shall be used only as a measure of last resort and for the shortest appropriate period of time;

c. Every child deprived of liberty shall be treated with humanity and respect for the inherent dignity of the human person, and in a manner which takes into account the needs of persons of his or her age. In particular, every child deprived of liberty shall be separated from adults unless it is considered in the child's best interest not to do so and shall have the right to maintain contact with his or her family through correspondence and visits, save in exceptional circumstances;

d. Every child deprived of his or her liberty shall have the right to prompt access to legal and other appropriate assistance, as well as the right to challenge the legality of the deprivation of his or her liberty before a court or other competent, independent and impartial authority, and to a prompt decision on any such action.

**Article 38**

1. States Parties undertake to respect and to ensure respect for rules of international humanitarian law applicable to them in armed conflicts which are relevant to the child.
2. States Parties shall take all feasible measures to ensure that persons who have not attained the age of fifteen years do not take a direct part in hostilities.
3. States Parties shall refrain from recruiting any person who has not attained the age of fifteen years into their armed forces. In recruiting among those persons who have attained the age of fifteen years but who have not attained the age of eighteen years, States Parties shall endeavour to give priority to those who are oldest.
4. In accordance with their obligations under international humanitarian law to protect the civilian population in armed conflicts, States Parties shall take all feasible measures to ensure protection and care of children who are affected by an armed conflict.

**Article 39**

States Parties shall take all appropriate measures to promote physical and psychological recovery and social reintegration of a child victim of: any form of neglect, exploitation, or abuse; torture or any other form of cruel, inhuman or degrading treatment or punishment; or armed conflicts. Such recovery and reintegration shall take place in an environment which fosters the health, self-respect and dignity of the child.

**Article 40**

1. States Parties recognize the right of every child alleged as, accused of, or recognized as having infringed the penal law to be treated in a manner consistent with the promotion of the child's sense of dignity and worth, which reinforces the child's respect for the human rights and fundamental freedoms of others and which takes into account the child's age and the desirability of promoting the child's reintegration and the child's assuming a constructive role in society.

2. To this end, and having regard to the relevant provisions of international instruments, States Parties shall, in particular, ensure that:

   a. No child shall be alleged as, be accused of, or recognized as having infringed the penal law by reason of acts or omissions that were not prohibited by national or international law at the time they were committed;

   b. Every child alleged as or accused of having infringed the penal law has at least the following guarantees:

      i. To be presumed innocent until proven guilty according to law;

      ii. To be informed promptly and directly of the charges against him or her, and, if appropriate, through his or her parents or legal guardians, and to have legal or other appropriate assistance in the preparation and presentation of his or her defence;

      iii. To have the matter determined without delay by a competent, independent and impartial authority or judicial body in a fair hearing according to law, in the presence of legal or other appropriate assistance and, unless it is considered not to be in the best interest of the child, in particular, taking into account his or her age or situation, his or her parents or legal guardians;

      iv. Not to be compelled to give testimony or to confess guilt; to examine or have examined adverse witnesses and to obtain the participation and examination of witnesses on his or her behalf under conditions of equality;

      v. If considered to have infringed the penal law, to have this decision and any measures imposed in consequence thereof reviewed by a higher competent, independent and impartial authority or judicial body according to law;

      vi. To have the free assistance of an interpreter if the child cannot understand or speak the language used;

      vii. To have his or her privacy fully respected at all stages of the proceedings.

3. States Parties shall seek to promote the establishment of laws, procedures, authorities and institutions specifically applicable to children alleged as, accused of, or recognized as having infringed the penal law, and, in particular:

   a. The establishment of a minimum age below which children shall be presumed not to have the capacity to infringe the penal law;

   b. Whenever appropriate and desirable, measures for dealing with such children without resorting to judicial proceedings, providing that human rights and legal safeguards are fully respected.

4. A variety of dispositions, such as care, guidance and supervision orders; counselling; probation; foster care; education and vocational training programmes and other alternatives to institutional care shall be available to ensure that children are dealt with in a manner appropriate to their well-being and proportionate both to their circumstances and the offence.

**Article 41**

Nothing in the present Convention shall affect any provisions which are more conducive to the realization of the rights of the child and which may be contained in:

a. The law of a State party; or

b. International law in force for that State.

## PART II

**Article 42**

States Parties undertake to make the principles and provisions of the Convention widely known, by appropriate and active means, to adults and children alike.

**Article 43**

1. For the purpose of examining the progress made by States Parties in achieving the realization of the obligations undertaken in the present Convention, there shall be established a Committee on the Rights of the Child, which shall carry out the functions hereinafter provided.
2. The Committee shall consist of ten experts of high moral standing and recognized competence in the field covered by this Convention. The members of the Committee shall be elected by States, Parties from among their nationals and shall serve in their personal capacity, consideration being given to equitable geographical distribution, as well as to the principal legal systems.
3. The members of the Committee shall be elected by secret ballot from a list of persons nominated by States Parties. Each State Party may nominate one person from among its own nationals.
4. The initial election to the Committee shall be held no later than six months after the date of the entry into force of the present Convention and thereafter every second year. At least four months before the date of each election, the Secretary-General of the United Nations shall address a letter to States, Parties inviting them to submit their nominations within two months. The Secretary-General shall subsequently prepare a list in alphabetical order of all persons thus nominated, indicating States Parties which have nominated them, and shall submit it to the States, Parties to the present Convention.
5. The elections shall be held at meetings of States Parties convened by the Secretary-General at United Nations Headquarters. At those meetings, for which two thirds of States Parties shall constitute a quorum, the persons elected to the Committee shall be those who obtain the largest number of votes and an absolute majority of the votes of the representatives of States Parties present and voting.
6. The members of the Committee shall be elected for a term of four years. They shall be eligible for re-election if renominated. The term of five of the members elected at the first election shall expire at the end of two years; immediately after the first election, the names of these five members shall be chosen by lot by the Chairman of the meeting.

7. If a member of the Committee dies or resigns or declares that for any other cause he or she can no longer perform the duties of the Committee, the State Party which nominated the member shall appoint another expert from among its nationals to serve for the remainder of the term, subject to the approval of the Committee.

8. The Committee shall establish its own rules of procedure.

9. The Committee shall elect its officers for a period of two years.

10. The meetings of the Committee shall normally be held at United Nations Headquarters or at any other convenient place as determined by the Committee. The Committee shall normally meet annually. The duration of the meetings of the Committee shall be determined, and reviewed, if necessary, by a meeting of the States Parties to the present Convention, subject to the approval of the General Assembly.

11. The Secretary-General of the United Nations shall provide the necessary staff and facilities for the effective performance of the functions of the Committee under the present Convention.

12. With the approval of the General Assembly, the members of the Committee established under the present Convention shall receive emoluments from United Nations resources on such terms and conditions as the Assembly may decide.

**Article 44**

1. States Parties undertake to submit to the Committee, through the Secretary-General of the United Nations, reports on the measures they have adopted which give effect to the rights recognized herein and on the progress made on the enjoyment of those rights:

   a. Within two years of the entry into force of the Convention for the State Party concerned;

   b. Thereafter every five years.

2. Reports made under the present article shall indicate factors and difficulties, if any, affecting the degree of fulfilment of the obligations under the present Convention. Reports shall also contain sufficient information to provide the Committee with a comprehensive understanding of the implementation of the Convention in the country concerned.

3. A State Party which has submitted a comprehensive initial report to the Committee need not, in its subsequent reports submitted in accordance with paragraph 1 (b) of the present article, repeat basic information previously provided.

4. The Committee may request from States, Parties further information relevant to the implementation of the Convention.

5. The Committee shall submit to the General Assembly, through the Economic and Social Council, every two years, reports on its activities.

6. States Parties shall make their reports widely available to the public in their own countries.

**Article 45**

In order to foster the effective implementation of the Convention and to encourage international co-operation in the field covered by the Convention:

1. The specialized agencies, the United Nations Children's Fund, and other United Nations organs shall be entitled to be represented at the consideration of the implementation of such provisions of the present Convention as fall within the scope of their mandate. The Committee may invite the specialized agencies, the United Nations Children's Fund and other competent bodies as it may consider appropriate to provide expert advice on the implementation of the Convention in areas falling within the scope of their respective mandates. The Committee may invite the specialized agencies, the United Nations Children's Fund, and other United Nations organs to submit reports on the implementation of the Convention in areas falling within the scope of their activities;
2. The Committee shall transmit, as it may consider appropriate, to the specialized agencies, the United Nations Children's Fund and other competent bodies, any reports from States Parties that contain a request, or indicate a need, for technical advice or assistance, along with the Committee's observations and suggestions, if any, on these requests or indications;
3. The Committee may recommend to the General Assembly to request the Secretary-General to undertake on its behalf studies on specific issues relating to the rights of the child;
4. The Committee may make suggestions and general recommendations based on information received pursuant to articles 44 and 45 of the present Convention. Such suggestions and general recommendations shall be transmitted to any State Party concerned and reported to the General Assembly, together with comments, if any, from States, Parties.

## PART III

**Article 46**

The present Convention shall be open for signature by all States.

**Article 47**

The present Convention is subject to ratification. Instruments of ratification shall be deposited with the Secretary-General of the United Nations.

**Article 48**

The present Convention shall remain open for accession by any State. The instruments of accession shall be deposited with the Secretary-General of the United Nations.

**Article 49**

1. The present Convention shall enter into force on the thirtieth day following the date of deposit with the Secretary-General of the United Nations of the twentieth instrument of ratification or accession.

2. For each State ratifying or acceding to the Convention after the deposit of the twentieth instrument of ratification or accession, the Convention shall enter into force on the thirtieth day after the deposit by such State of its instrument of ratification or accession.

**Article 50**

1. Any State Party may propose an amendment and file it with the Secretary-General of the United Nations. The Secretary-General shall thereupon communicate the proposed amendment to States, Parties, with a request that they indicate whether they favour a conference of States, Parties for the purpose of considering and voting upon the proposals. In the event that, within four months from the date of such communication, at least one third of the States, Parties favour such a conference, the Secretary-General shall convene the conference under the auspices of the United Nations. Any amendment adopted by a majority of States, Parties present and voting at the conference shall be submitted to the General Assembly for approval.
2. An amendment adopted in accordance with paragraph 1 of the present article shall enter into force when it has been approved by the General Assembly of the United Nations and accepted by a two-thirds majority of States, Parties.
3. When an amendment enters into force, it shall be binding on those States Parties which have accepted it, other States, Parties still being bound by the provisions of the present Convention and any earlier amendments which they have accepted.

**Article 51**

1. The Secretary-General of the United Nations shall receive and circulate to all States the text of reservations made by States at the time of ratification or accession.
2. A reservation incompatible with the object and purpose of the present Convention shall not be permitted.
3. Reservations may be withdrawn at any time by notification to that effect addressed to the Secretary-General of the United Nations, who shall then inform all States. Such notification shall take effect on the date on which it is received by the Secretary-General

**Article 52**

A State Party may denounce the present Convention by written notification to the Secretary-General of the United Nations. Denunciation becomes effective one year after the date of receipt of the notification by the Secretary-General.

**Article 53**

The Secretary-General of the United Nations is designated as the depositary of the present Convention.

**Article 54**

The original of the present Convention, of which the Arabic, Chinese, English, French, Russian and Spanish texts are equally authentic, shall be deposited with the Secretary-General of the United Nations.

IN WITNESS THEREOF the undersigned plenipotentiaries, being duly authorized thereto by their respective governments, have signed the present Convention.

**Given below is the child friendly version of the Convention for easier understanding**

## CONVENTION ON CHILD RIGHTS (CHILD-FRIENDLY VERSION)

**Article 1: Definition of the child**

Every human being below 18 years unless majority is attained earlier according to the law applicable to the child.

**Article 2: Non discrimination**

All rights must be granted to each child without exception. The State must protect the child without exception. The State must protect the child against all forms of discriminations.

**Article 3: Best interests of the child**

In all actions concerning children, the best interest of the child shall be the major consideration.

**Article 4: Implementation of rights**

The obligation on the State to ensure that the rights in the Convention are implemented.

**Article 5: Parents, family, community rights and responsibilities**

States are to respect the parents and family in their child rearing function.

**Article 6: Life, survival and development**

The right of the child to life and the state's obligation to ensure the child's survival and development.

**Article 7: Name and nationality**

The right from birth to a name, to acquire a nationality and to know and be cared for by his or her parents.

**Article 8: Preservation of identity**

The obligation of the State to assist the child in reestablishing identity if this has been illegally withdrawn.

**Article 9: Non-separation from parents**

The right of the child to retain contact with his parents in cases of separation. If separation is the result of detention, imprisonment or death the State shall provide the information to the child or parents about the whereabouts of the missing family member.

**Article 10: Family reunification**

Requests to leave or enter country for family reunification shall be dealt with in a human manner. A child has the right to maintain regular contacts with both parents when they live in different States.

**Article 11: Illicit transfer and non-return of children**

The State shall combat child kidnapping by a partner or third party.

**Article 12: Expression of opinion**

The right of the child to express his or her opinion and to have this taken into consideration.

**Article 13: Freedom of expression and information**

The right to seek, receive and impart information in various forms, including art, print, writing.

**Article 14: Freedom of thought, conscience and religion**

States are to be respect the rights and duties of parents to provide direction to the child in the exercise of this right in accordance with the child's evolving capacities.

**Article 15: Freedom of association**

The child's right to freedom of association and peaceful assembly.

**Article 16: Privacy, honour, reputation**

No child shall be subjected to interference with privacy, family, home or correspondence.

**Article 17: Access to information and media**

The child shall have access to information from a diversity of sources; due attention shall be paid to minorities and guidelines to protect children from harmful material shall be encouraged.

**Article 18: Parental responsibility**

Both parents have common responsibilities for the upbringing of the child and assistance shall be given to them in the performance of the parental responsibilities.

**Article 19: Abuse and neglect (while in family or care)**

States have the obligation to protect children from all forms of abuse. Social programmes and support services shall be made available.

**Article 20: Alternative care for children in the absence of parents**

The entitlement of the child to alternative care with national laws and the obligation on the State to pay due regard to continuity in the child's religious, cultural, linguistic or ethnic background in the provision of alternative care.

**Article 21: Adoption**

States are to ensure that only authorised bodies carry out adoption. Inter-country adoption may be considered if national solutions have been exhausted.

**Article 22: Refugee children**

Special protection is to be given to refugee children. States shall cooperate with international agencies to this end and also reunite children separated from the families.

**Article 23: Disabled children**

The right to benefit from special care and education for a fuller life in society.

**Article 24: Health care**

Access to preventive and curative health care services as well as the gradual abolition of traditional practices harmful to the child.

**Article 25: Periodic review**

The child who is placed for care, protection or treatment has the right to have the placement reviewed on a regular basis.

**Article 26: Social security**

The child's right to social security

**Article 27: Standard of living**

Parental responsibility to provide adequate living conditions for the child's development even when one of the parents is living in a country other than the child's place of residence.

**Article 28: Education**

The right to free primary education, the availability of vocational education, and the need for measures to reduce the drop-out rates.

**Article 29: Aims of education**

Education should foster the development of the child's personality and talents, preparation for a responsible adult life, respect for human rights as well as the cultural and national values of the child's country and that of others.

**Article 30: Children of minorities and indigenous children**

The right of the child belonging to a minority or indigenous group to enjoy his or her culture, to practise his or her own language.

**Article 31: Play and recreation**

The right of the child to play, recreational activities and to participate in cultural and artistic life.

**Article 32: Economic exploitation**

The right of the child to protection against harmful forms of work and against exploitation.

**Article 33: Narcotic and psychotic substances**

Protection of the child from their illicit use and the utilisation of the child in their production and distribution.

**Article 34: Sexual exploitation**

Protection of the child from sexual exploitation including prostitution and the use of children in pornographic materials

**Article 35: Abduction, sale and traffic**

State obligation to prevent the abduction, sale of or traffic in children.

**Article 36: Other forms of exploitation**

**Article 37: Torture, capital punishment, deprivation of liberty**

Obligation of the State *vis-a-vis* children in detention.

**Article 38: Armed conflicts**

Children under 15 years are not to take a direct part in hostilities. No recruitment of children under 15 years.

**Article 39: Recovery and reintegration**

State obligations for the reeducation and social reintegration of child victims of exploitation, torture or armed conflicts.

**Article 40: Juvenile justice**

Treatment of child accused of infringing the penal law shall promote the child's sense of dignity.

**Article 41: Rights of the child in other instruments**

**Article 42: Dissemination of the Convention**

The state's duty to make the convention known to adults and children.

**Article 43-54: Implementation**

These paragraphs provide for a Committee on the Rights of the Child to oversee implementation of the Convention.

[The titles of articles are for ease of reference only. They do not form part of the adopted text. (UNICEF - UK)]

☆☆☆☆☆

# 4 CHAPTER

# CHILD ABUSE

**"Safety and security don't just happen; they are the result of collective consensus and public investment. We owe our children, the most vulnerable citizens in our society, a life free of violence and fear."** **—*Nelson Mandela***

Child abuse is a state of emotional, physical, economic and sexual maltreatment meted out to a person below the age of eighteen and is a globally prevalent phenomenon. However, in India, as in many other countries, there has been no understanding of the extent, magnitude and trends of the problem. The growing complexities of life and the dramatic changes brought about by socio-economic transitions in India have played a major role in increasing the vulnerability of children to various and newer forms of abuse.

Child abuse has serious physical and psycho-social consequences which adversely affect the health and overall well-being of a child. According to World Health Organisation [WHO]: "Child abuse or maltreatment constitutes all forms of physical and/or emotional ill-treatment, sexual abuse, neglect or negligent treatment or commercial or other exploitation, resulting in actual or potential harm to the child's health, survival, development or dignity in the context of a relationship of responsibility, trust or power.''

Child abuse is a violation of the basic human rights of a child and is an outcome of a set of inter-related familial, social, psychological and economic factors. The problem of child abuse and human rights violations is one of the most critical matters on the international human rights agenda. In the Indian context acceptance of child rights as primary inviolable rights is fairly recent, as is the universal understanding of it.

## DEFINITION OF CHILD ABUSE

The term 'Child Abuse' may have different connotations in different cultural milieu and socio-economic situations.

Child abuse refers to the intended, unintended and perceived maltreatment of the child, whether habitual or not, including any of the following: - physical abuse, sexual abuse, emotional abuse and neglect. It includes any act, deed or word which debases, degrades or demeans the intrinsic worth and dignity of a child.

**Physical Abuse:** Physical abuse is the inflicting of physical injury upon a child. This may include burning, hitting, punching, shaking, kicking, beating or otherwise harming a child. The parent or caretaker may not have intended to hurt the child. It may, however, be the result of over-discipline or physical punishment that is inappropriate to the child's age.

**Sexual Abuse:** Sexual abuse is inappropriate sexual behaviour with a child. It includes fondling a child's genitals, making the child fondle the adult's genitals, intercourse, incest, rape, sodomy, exhibitionism, pornography and sexual exploitation. To be considered 'child abuse', these acts have to be committed by a person responsible for the care of a child (for example a baby-sitter, a parent, or a daycare provider), or related to the child. If a stranger commits these acts, it would be considered sexual assault and handled solely by the police and criminal courts.

**Emotional Abuse:** Emotional abuse is also known as verbal abuse, mental abuse, and psychological maltreatment. It includes acts or the failures to act by parents or caretakers that have caused or could cause, serious behavioural, cognitive, emotional, or mental trauma. This can include parents/caretakers using extreme and/or bizarre forms of punishment, such as confinement in a closet or dark room or being tied to a chair for long periods of time or threatening or terrorizing a child. Less severe acts, but no less damaging, are belittling or rejecting treatment, using derogatory terms to describe the child, habitual tendency to blame the child or make him/her a scapegoat.

**Neglect:** It is the failure to provide for the child's basic needs. Neglect can be physical, educational, or emotional. Physical neglect can include not providing adequate food or clothing, appropriate medical care, supervision, or proper weather protection (heat or cold). It may include abandonment. Educational neglect includes failure to provide appropriate schooling or special educational needs, allowing excessive truancies. Psychological neglect includes the lack of any emotional support and love, never attending to the child, substance abuse including allowing the child to participate in drug and alcohol use.

## PHYSICAL INDICATORS OF ABUSE IN THE CHILD

- bite marks
- unusual bruises
- lacerations
- burns
- high incidence of accidents or frequent injuries
- fractures in unusual places
- injuries, swellings to face and extremities
- discoloration of skin

## BEHAVIOURAL INDICATORS OF ABUSE IN THE CHILD

- avoids physical contact with others
- apprehensive when other children cry
- wears clothing to purposely conceal injury, i.e. long sleeves
- refuses to undress for gym or for required physical exams at school
- gives inconsistent versions about occurrence of injuries, burns, etc.
- seems frightened by parents
- often late or absent from school
- comes early to school, seems reluctant to go home afterwards
- has difficulty in getting along with others,
- little respect for others

## PARENTAL/FAMILIAL INDICATORS IN ABUSIVE FAMILIES

- many personal and marital problems
- economic stress
- parent(s) were abused as children themselves, were raised in homes where excessive punishment was the norm, and use harsh discipline on own children
- highly moralistic
- history of alcohol or drug abuse
- are easily upset, have a low tolerance for frustration
- are antagonistic, suspicious and fearful of other people
- social isolation, no supporting network of relatives or friends
- see child as bad or evil.
- little or no interest in child's wellbeing;

## CHILD ABUSE ACROSS THE GLOBE

WHO estimates that almost 53,000 child deaths in 2002 were due to child homicide. In the Global School-based Student Health Survey carried out in a wide range of developing countries, between 20% and 65% of school going children reported having been verbally or physically bullied in school in the previous 30 days. Similar rates of bullying have been found in industrialised countries.

An estimated 150 million girls and 73 million boys under 18 have experienced forced sexual intercourse or other forms of sexual violence involving physical contact.

UNICEF estimates that in sub-Saharan Africa, Egypt and Sudan, 3 million girls and women are subjected to female genital mutilation every year.

ILO estimates that 218 million children were involved in child labour in 2004, of whom 126 million were engaged in hazardous work.

Estimates from 2000 suggest that 5.7 million children were in forced or bonded labour, 1.8 million in prostitution and pornography and 1.2 million were victims of trafficking.

Only 2.4% of the world's children are legally protected from corporal punishment in all settings.

## CHILD ABUSE IN ASIA

While certain child abuse and neglect issues are common in almost all countries at the global level such as physical abuse, sexual abuse, emotional and psychological abuse, abandonment and, increasingly, problems of street children, there are also many issues which are prevalent only in certain regions of the world. For instance, in Asia where population density is high, the issues of child labour and child sexual exploitation are also high. Political instability and other internal disturbances, including conditions of insurgency in many countries in Asia are also creating major problems, with increasing number of child soldiers, refugee children, trafficked children and children on the streets.

Prevention of child abuse and neglect is still an uncharted field in Asia. The largest population of children in the world live in South Asia and majority of these children lack access to proper health care, nutrition and education. This reflects the socio-economic reality of the developing countries of the Asian region. The main factors that contribute to the magnitude of the problem of child abuse are poverty, illiteracy, caste system and landlessness, lack of economic opportunities, rural-urban migration, population growth, political instability and weak implementation of legal provisions.

Mostly, the approaches for prevention and methods of treatment of child abuse do not cover the entire gamut of abuse. Lack of reliable data on the incidence of child abuse and of knowledge of methods of prevention and treatment has been recognized and is being addressed by sovereign governments, national and international organizations, e.g., UNICEF, Save the Children, Plan International, International Society for Prevention of Child Abuse and Neglect (ISPCAN, ) etc.

## CHILD ABUSE IN INDIA

The Indian society, like most societies across the world, is patriarchal in structure where the chain of command is definite and inviolable. In such power structures parents, both fathers and mothers, consider their children as their property and assume a freedom to treat them as they like. Thus, not only do parents and teachers adopt harsh methods of disciplining children, there is also little opposition to this harshness. The underlying belief is that physical punishment encourages discipline in children and is for their betterment in the long-run. There is enough scientific proof to the contrary and evidence suggests that sometimes it is parent's inability to raise their children, and their frustrations find a manifestation in the form of beating them or causing other physical harm.

Severe physical maltreatment also takes place outside family situations and the most common and known forms of it are corporal punishment in schools and physical abuse at work place. Working children have a high probability of being abused by their employer or supervisor. The reasons could be dependence of the child on the employer and the vulnerability of the child, who is a soft and available target for the anger and frustrations of the employer. The same goes with teachers in schools and every other person resorting to physical abuse of children. Whether it is called disciplining or venting of personal frustrations, the fact is that it is a grave violation of children's right to live with dignity and freedom from violence, their right to be loved and cared for and their right to be nurtured with respect.

Nineteen percent of the world's children live in India. According to the 2001 Census, some 440 million people in the country today are aged below eighteen years and constitute 42 per cent of India's total population, i.e., four out of every ten persons. This is an enormous number of children that the country has to take care of. While articulating its vision of progress, development and equity, India has expressed its recognition of the fact that when its children are educated, healthy, happy and have access to opportunities, they are the country's greatest human resource.

The National Policy for Children, 1974, declared children to be a 'supreme national asset'. It pledged measures to secure and safeguard all their needs, declaring that this could be done by making wise use of available national resources. Unfortunately, ten successive Five Year Plans have not allocated adequate resources to meet the needs of children. An exercise on child budgeting carried out by the Ministry of Women and Child Development revealed that total expenditure on children in 2005-2006 in health, education, development and protection together amounted to a mere 3.86%, rising to 4.91% in 2006-07. However, the share of resources for child protection was abysmally low at 0.034% in 2005-06 and remained the same in 2006-07. Available resources have also not been utilized effectively for achieving outcomes for children. As a result, the status and condition of children have remained far from secure.

Harmful traditional practices like child marriage, caste system, discrimination against the girl child, child labour and Devadasi tradition impact negatively on children and increase their vulnerability to abuse and neglect. Lack of adequate nutrition, poor access to medical and educational facilities, migration from rural to urban areas leading to rise in urban poverty, children on the streets and child beggars, all result in break down of families. These increase the vulnerabilities of children and expose them to situations of abuse and exploitation.

According to the report published in 2005 on 'Trafficking in Women and Children in India', 44,476 children were reported missing in India, out of which 11,008 children continued to remain untraced. India, being a major source and destination country for trafficked children from within India and adjoining countries has, by conservative estimates, three to five lakh girl children in commercial sex and organized prostitution.

## STUDY ON CHILD ABUSE: INDIA 2007

- Every fifth child in the world lives in India
- Every third malnourished child in the world lives in India
- Every second Indian child is underweight
- Three out of four children in India are anemic
- Every second new born has reduced learning capacity due to iodine deficiency
- Decline in female/male ratio is maximum in 0-6 years: 927 females per 1000 males
- Birth registration is just 62%
- Retention rate at Primary level is 71.01% (Elementary Education in India Progress towards Universal Elementary Education (UEE), NUEPA (National University of Educational Planning and Administration) Flash Statistics DISE (District Information System for Education) 2005-2006)
- Girls' enrolment in schools at primary level is 47.79% (Elementary Education in India Progress towards UEE, NUEPA Flash Statistics DISE 2005-2006)
- 1104 lakh child labour in the country
- IMR[Infant Mortality Rate] is as high as 58 per 1000 live births
- MMR [Maternal Mortality Rate] is equally high at 301 per 100,000 live births
- Children born with low birth weight are 46%
- Children under 3 with anemia are 79%
- Immunization coverage is very low (polio - 78.2%, measles -58.8%, DPT-55.3%, BCG-78%

## CHILD SURVIVAL AND CHILD HEALTH IN INDIA

2.5 million children die in India every year, accounting for one in five deaths in the world, with girls being 50% more likely to die. One out of 16 children die before they attain one year of age, and one out of 11 die before they attain five years of age. India accounts for 35% of the developing world's low birth weight babies and 40% of child malnutrition in developing countries, one of the highest levels in the world. Although India's neo-natal mortality rate declined in the 1990s from 69 per 1000 live births in 1980 to 53 per 1000 live births in 1990, it remained static, dropping only four points from 48 to 44 per 1000 live births between

1995 and 2000. The 2001 Census data and other studies illustrate the terrible impact of sex selection in India over the last few decades. The child sex ratio (0-6 years) declined from 945 girls to 1000 boys in 1991 to 927 in the 2001 Census.

India has the second highest national total of persons living with HIV/AIDS after the Republic of South Africa. According to National Aids Control Organization (NACO), there were an estimated 0.55 lakh HIV infected 0-14 year old children in India in 2003. UNAIDS, however, puts this figure at 0.16 million children. According to the 2001 Census report, amongst all persons living with disabilities, 35.9% were children and young adults in the 0-19 age group. Three out of five children in the age group of 0-9 years have been reported to be visually impaired. Movement disability has the highest proportion (33.2%) in the age group of 10-19 years. This is largely true of mental disability also.

## CHILD PROTECTION

While on the one hand girls are being killed even before they are born, on the other hand children who are born and survive suffer from a number of violations. The world's highest number of working children is in India. To add to this, India has the world's largest number of sexually abused children, with

- a child below 10 every 13th hour and
- one in every 10 children sexually abused at any point of time.

The National Crime Records Bureau (NCRB) reported 14,975 cases of various crimes against children in 2005 .

Most subtle forms of violence against children such as child marriage, economic exploitation, practices like the 'Devadasi' tradition of dedicating young girls to gods and goddesses, genital mutilation in some parts of the country are often rationalized on grounds of culture and tradition.

Physical and psychological punishments take place in the name of disciplining children and are culturally accepted. Forced evictions, displacement due to development projects, war and conflict, communal riots, natural disasters — all of these take their own toll on children.

## CHILD PARTICIPATION

Children in most sections of Indian society are traditionally and conventionally not consulted about matters and decisions affecting their lives. In the family and household, the neighbourhood and wider community, in school or in work place, and across the settings of social and cultural life, children's views are mostly not given much importance. If they do speak out, they are not normally heard. The imposition of restrictive norms is especially true for girl children. This limits children's access to information and to choice, and often to the possibility of seeking help outside their immediate circle.

## STATUS OF CHILDREN

As discussed above, there is a large child population in India and a large percentage of this population is vulnerable to abuse, exploitation and neglect. There is also inadequate information about the extent of child abuse in the country. Barring a few sporadic studies, with limited scope, the attempt to understand the different forms and magnitude of child abuse across the country has been inadequate. The only information available annually is the crime data maintained by NCRB*

A look at the data maintained by NCRB shows that:

1. There is a record of only those crimes which can be registered under the IPC or other criminal Acts.
2. Corporal punishment, use of children for creation of pornography, exposure, etc., are not reflected in NCRB data as they are not offences under the IPC.

| Crime Head | 2002 | 2003 | 2004 | 2005 |
|---|---|---|---|---|
| Rape | 2532 | 2949 | 3542 | 4026 |
| Kidnapping & Abduction | 2322 | 2571 | 3196 | 3518 |
| Procurement of Minor Girls | 124 | 171 | 205 | 145 |
| Selling of Girls for Prostitution | 5 | 36 | 19 | 50 |
| Infanticide | 115 | 103 | 102 | 108 |
| Foeticide | 84 | 57 | 86 | 86 |

[* National Crime Records Bureau, Ministry of Home Affairs, Govt. of India (2005): Crime in India]

There is a gross under-reporting of crimes against children, which in itself is indicative of the low priority accorded to children by parents, caregivers and the police.

☆☆☆☆☆

5

CHAPTER

# CHILD WELFARE ACTIVITIES IN INDIA

**"Children do not constitute anyone's property: they are neither the property of their parents nor even of society. They belong only to their own future freedom."**

***—Mikhail Bakunin***

Children constitute principle assets of any country. Children's Development is as important as the development of material resources and the best way to develop national human resources is to take care of children. India has the largest child population in the world. Significant progress has been made in many fields in assuring children their basic rights. However, much remains to be done. The country renews its commitment and determination to give the highest priority to the basic needs and rights of all children. Children are most vulnerable to exploitation and abuse. A lot more has to be done for the health, nutrition and education of children. It is unfortunate that girls in particular face debilitating discrimination at all stages. Therefore, specific concentration is being given to the efforts to improve the life and opportunities of the Girl Child.

## LEGISLATIONS

There are several Legislations pertaining to children. These include the following-

1. The Child Marriage Restraint Act, 1929.
2. The Child Labour (Prohibition and Regulation) Act, 1986.
3. The Juvenile Justice (Care and Protection of Children) Act, 2000.
4. The Infant Milk Substitutes, Feeding Bottles and Infant Foods (Regulation of Production, Supply and Distribution) Act, 1992.
5. The Pre-conception and Pre-natal Diagnostic Technique (Prohibition of Sex Selection) Act, 1994.
6. The Persons with Disabilities (Equal Opportunities, Protection of Rights and Full Participation) Act, 1995.
7. The Immoral Traffic (Prevention) Act, 1956.

8. The Guardian and Wards Act, 1890.
9. The Young Persons (Harmful Publications) Act, 1956.
10. The Commissions for Protection of Child Rights Act, 2005.

**The National Policy for Children** was adopted on 22nd Aug., 1974. This Policy lays down that the State shall provide adequate services towards children, both before and after birth and during the growing stages for their full physical, mental and social development. The measures suggested include amongst others, a comprehensive health programme, supplementary nutrition for mothers and children, free and compulsory education for all children up to the age of 14 years, promotion of physical education and recreational activities, special consideration for children of weaker sections like SCs and STs, prevention of exploitation of children, etc.

The Government of India adopted the **National Charter for Children** which has been prepared after obtaining the views/comments and suggestions of the State Governments/UT Administrations, concerned Ministries and Departments and experts in the field. The National Charter is a statement of intent embodying the Government's agenda for children. The document emphasizes Government of India's commitment to children's rights to survival, health and nutrition, standard of living, play and leisure, early childhood care, education, protection of the girl child, empowering adolescents, equality, life and liberty, name and nationality, freedom of expression, freedom of association and peaceful assembly, the right to a family and the right to be protected from economic exploitation and all forms of abuse. The document also provides for protection of children in difficult circumstances, children with disabilities, children from marginalised and disadvantaged communities, and child victims. The document while stipulating the duties of the State and the Community towards children also emphasizes the duties of children towards family, society and the Nation. The National Charter for Children was notified in the Gazette of India on 9th Feb., 2004.

India acceded to the UN Convention on the Rights of the Child on 11th Dec., 1992 to reiterate its commitment to the cause of children. The objective of the Convention is to give every child the right to survival and development in a healthy and congenial environment.

India is also party to the **Millennium Development Goals** and the **SAARC Conventions on Child Welfare** and **Combating Trafficking of Women and Children in SAARC Region**.

**National Plan of Action for Children 2005,** the Ministry of Women and Child Development has prepared a National Plan of Action for Children 2005 after harmonizing the goals for children set in the UN General Assembly Special Session on Children held in 2002 and the monitorable targets set in the Tenth Five Year Plan, and goals for children in related Ministries/Departments. The Action Plan has been prepared in consultation with concerned Ministries and Departments, States/Union Territory Governments, Non Governmental Organizations and experts. The National Plan of Action includes goals, objectives, strategies and activities for improving nutritional status of children, reducing Infant Mortality Rate (IMR) and Maternal Mortality Rate, (MMR) increasing enrolment ratio and reducing dropout rates, universalization of primary education, increasing coverage for immunization etc. The Prime Minister's Office is quarterly monitoring the National Plan of Action for Children 2005 on the basis of eight parameters. These are as under:

1. Reduce IMR to below 30 per 1000 live births by 2010.
2. Reduce Child Mortality Rate to below 31 per 1000 live births by 2010.
3. Reduce Maternal Mortality Rate to below 100 per 100,000 live births by 2010.
4. Universal equitable access and use of safe drinking water and improved access to sanitary means of excreta disposal by 2010.
5. 100% rural population to have access to basic sanitation by 2012.
6. Eliminate child marriages by 2010
7. Eliminate disability due to poliomyelitis by 2007
8. Reduce the proportion of infants infected with HIV by 20 percent by 2007 and by 50 percent by 2010, by ensuring that 80 per cent of pregnant women have access to ante natal care, and 95 per cent of men and women aged 15-24 have access to care, counseling and other HIV and prevention services.

## SCHEMES/PROJECTS

Several Ministries and Departments of the Government of India are implementing various schemes and programmes for the benefit of children. Some of the Schemes and Programmes being implemented by the Ministry of Women and Child Development are as under:

**Integrated Child Development Services (ICDS) Scheme—**

- ***Rajiv Gandhi National Creche Scheme:*** for the children of working mothers The Ministry of Women and Child Development has launched a new Creche Scheme w.e.f. 1.1.2006 by merging the National Creche Fund with the Scheme of Assistance to Voluntary Organisations for Creche for Working and Ailing Women's Children and also to revise the financial norms from Rs.18,480/- to Rs. 42,384/- per crèche per annum. The Scheme provides crèche services to the children of age group of 0 to 6 year, which includes supplementary nutrition, emergency medicines and contingency. The Scheme has been named as *Rajiv Gandhi National Creche Scheme for the Children of Working Mothers.* These crèches will be allocated to the Central Social Welfare Board, Indian Council for Child Welfare and Bhartiya Adim Jati Sevak Sangh in the ratio of 80:11:9. The priority will be given to uncovered districts/areas and tribal areas while extending the scheme to maintain balance regional coverage. Eligibility criteria under the Revised Scheme has also been enhanced from Rs 1800/- to Rs.12,000/- per month per family. So far about 25,605 creches have been sanctioned including 5,137 creches sanctioned under erstwhile National Creche Scheme upto 20th Nov., 2006

Nutrition Component of Prime Minister Gramodya Yojana and Nutrition Programme for Adolescent Girls in 51 Districts being implemented with additional central assistance given by the Planning Commission, directly and indirectly contribute to promoting nutrition of children. A National Nutrition Mission has been set up under the chairpersonship of Hon'ble Prime Minister *vide* notification dated 31st July 2003 with a view to enable policy direction to concerned Departments of the Government for addressing the problem of malnutrition in a mission mode.

- **An Integrated Programme for Street Children:** is being implemented by the Ministry of Women and Child Development specifically for those children who are on streets and homeless and include the ragpicking and vagabond children. The Scheme aims at providing full and wholesome development of children without homes and family ties. The children without homes and family ties and children especially vulnerable to abuse and exploitation such as children of sex workers and children of pavement dwellers are the target group for this Programme. Financial assistance is provided to the NGOs who are eligible and working for the welfare of the street children, for Formal and Non-formal Education, Shelter Home, Vocational Training to Children, Nutrition, health care, sanitation and hygiene, safe drinking water, education and recreational facilities and protection against abuse and exploitation.
- **Integrated Programme for Juvenile Justice:** The programme is being implemented by the Ministry of Social Justice and Empowerment with a view to providing care to children in difficult circumstances and children in conflict with the law through Government institutions and through NGOs. Some special features of the scheme areas:

- Establishment of a National Advisory Board on Juvenile Justice (JJ)
- Creation of a Juvenile Justice Fund.
- Training, orientation and sensitization of Judicial, administrative police and NGOs responsible for implementation of JJ Act.
- Institutional care shall be used but only as a last measure by enlarging the range of suitable alternatives.
- Financial assistance to bring about a qualitative improvement in the existing infrastructure.
- Expansion of non-institutional services such as sponsorship, foster care, probation, etc., as and an alternate to institutional care.

- **Childline India Foundation (CIF):** has been set up as a nodal organization, supported by Government of India, to monitor and ensure the qualitative development of the Childline service across the country. Childline is a toll free telephone service (1098) which anyone can call for assistance in the interest of children. It has prescribed minimum quality standards for the services to be provided by its partner organizations that are implementing Childline programmes in various cities of the country. It initiates preparatory activity that precedes the initiation of Childline service in any city. CIF is also involved in awareness and advocacy in order to strengthen the efforts relating to child welfare.

The objective of the Shishu Greh Scheme is to promote adoptions within the country and to ensure minimum standards in the care of abandoned/orphaned/destitute children. Grant-in-Aid upto a ceiling of Rs.6 lakh has been provided per unit of 10 children in a Shishu Greh.

## RECENT INITIATIVES

**The Commissions for Protection of the Child Rights Act 2005—** The Government has recently notified the Commissions for Protection of Child Rights Act 2005 in the Gazette of India on 20th Jan., 2006 as Act No. 4 of 2006. The Act envisages setting up a National Commission at the National level and the State Commissions at the State level. The proposed Commission would be set up for proper enforcement of children's rights and effective implementation of laws and programmes relating to children. The National Commission for Protection of Child Rights will be a statutory body to be set up under the Commissions for Protection of Child Rights Act. The proposed Commission will have a Chairperson and six other Members, including two women members, a Member Secretary and other supporting staff. The Chairperson would be a person of eminence in the field of child development. The members would be the experts in the field of child health, education, child care and development, juvenile justice, children with disabilities, elimination of child labour, child psychology or sociology and laws relating to children. The officers and the staff of the Commission will be provided by the Central Government. The proposed Commission would be set up for proper enforcement of children's rights and effective implementation of laws and programmes relating to children.

### The Functions of the Commissions:

- Examine and review the safeguards provided by Constitution or any law for the protection of child rights and recommend measures for their effective implementation
- Present to the Central Government, annually, reports upon the working of those safeguards.
- Examine all factors that inhibit the enjoyment of rights of most vulnerable children and children in need of special care and protection
- Study treaties and other international instruments and undertake periodical review of existing policies, programmes and other activities on child rights and make recommendation for their effective implementation in the best interest of children.
- Undertake and promote research in the field of child rights
- Spread child rights literacy among various sections of the society and promote awareness
- Inspect any juvenile custodial home, or any other place of residence or institution meant for children for the purpose of treatment, reformation or protection and take up with these authorities for remedial action
- Inquire into complaints and take *suo motu* notice of matters relating to,-

  i. deprivation of child's rights;

  ii. non-implementation of laws for protection and development of children;

  iii. non-compliance of policy decisions, guidelines or and to provide relief to such children,
- Or take up the issues arising out of such matters with appropriate authorities; and
- Such other functions as it may consider necessary for the promotion of child rights

### The Powers of the Commission include the following:

a. summoning and enforcing the attendance of any person and examining him on oath;

b. requiring the discovery and production of any document;

c. receiving evidence on affidavits;

d. requisitioning any public record or copy thereof from any court or office;

e. issuing summons for the examination of witnesses and documents;

f. forwarding any case to a Magistrate having jurisdiction to try the same and the Magistrate to whom any such case is forwarded shall proceed to hear the complaint against the accused;

g. recommending to the concerned Government or authority the initiation of proceedings for prosecution or such other action as deem fit against the concerned person/s;

h. approaching the Supreme Court or the High Court concerned for such directions, orders or writs as that Court may deem necessary;

i. recommending to the concerned Government or authority for the grant of such interim relief to the victim or the members of his family as the Commission consider necessary.

### State Commissions for Protection of Child Rights:

The Bill also provides that State Governments may constitute State Commissions for Protection of Child Rights in their State and designate a State level and other district level children's Court in their respective State. The Bill has similar provisions for State Commissions in respect of their constitution, reporting, functions and powers.

With the alleviation of the status of Department of Women and Child Development to an independent Ministry headed by the Minister of State having independent charge it was necessary to change the above provision to make the Minister in charge of the Ministry or Department of Women and Child Development as the Chairperson of the Selection Committee for the selection of the Chairperson of the National Commission for Protection of Child Rights. Hence, the Commissions for Protection of Child Rights (Amendment) Bill 2006 was prepared which has been passed by both the Houses of Parliament in the Winter Session. The Commission will be set up once the above Amendment Bill is assented to by the President which would enable the Ministry of Women and Child Development to select the Chairperson and Members of the Commission for its constitution.

The initiatives are being taken for constitution of the National Commission for Protection of Child Rights. The Rules for implementation of the provisions of the Act in respect for National Commission for Protection of Child Rights have been notified on 31.7.2006. Ministry of Finance have also approved certain number of posts for the National Commission. Initiatives have been taken for appointment of Member Secretary and staff for the National Commission.

## Offences Against Children (Prevention) Bill

Child abuse involves several aspects, such as, sexual exploitation, economic exploitation, domestic violence, trafficking for prostitution, corporal punishment at school, and others. Therefore, the Ministry felt a need to have a dialogue on the issue so as to ascertain the views from all quarters and to formulate a consensus in order to address the issue more adequately and effectively. Accordingly few consultations have been made with voluntary organizations and experts dealing with the subject. It has been decided after consultation to constitute a small group consisting of representative from Government, NGOs, legal experts and social workers which will go into all aspects of the subject and after considering all existing legal provisions and others available on the subject and formulate a draft legislation to address all issues pertaining to child abuse. After wide consultations a draft Bill for Offences Against Children was prepared and circulated to the State Governments for their comments and views. After obtaining the comments of concerned Ministries and Departments a draft Cabinet Note has been referred to Law Ministry for their vetting.The proposal will be placed before the Cabinet shortly.

### Child Budgeting

The key objectives of the endeavor would be to analyse budgetary provisions on social sector, to identify the magnitude of budgetary allocations made by the Centre/State Governments on schemes meant for addressing specific needs of children, to examine the trend in child specific expenditure etc. The main agenda for the exercise of child budgeting is to review resource allocations related to children; explore ways to increase budgetary allocations for children; assess budget utilization rates for social sector and child specific programmes, identify blockages and constraints to effective utilization; identify methods for tracking expenditure and monitoring performance to ensure that outlays translate into outcomes for children

**Proposed Integrated Programme for Child Services.** As per the 2001 Census, there were 427 million children in the country. There are millions of children living in the difficult circumstances. The child protection programme in India is shared between various Ministries, which have been implementing the schemes and programmes to reach out to varied groups of vulnerable children with complex and diverse needs. The important schemes and programmes for such children include **Programme for Juvenile Justice, Integrated Programme for Street Children, Shishu Griha Scheme, Scheme for Working Children in Need of Care and Protection, General Grant-in-Aid Scheme, CHILDLINE Service, Rajiv Gandhi National crèche scheme for the children of Working mothers, Pilot Project to Combat the Trafficking of Women and Children for Commercial Sexual Exploitation in Destination Areas**, etc. However, experiences with the implementation of existing programmes and polices has brought out a large number of shortcomings in the system.

In view of the gaps identified and recommendations and suggestions received from various quarters it has decided to combine the existing child protection schemes under one integrated scheme titled "Integrated Child Protection Scheme". The proposed scheme aims to provide for care and protection of all the children in conflict with law and children in need of care and protection. It would involve steps to strengthen families and prevent them to breakup leading children to become homeless and without care and protection. At the same time, children already outside the mainstream need to be provided support beginning from emergency outreach services to final rehabilitation with their families/society. Details of the Scheme are being worked out which is proposed to be implemented in the Eleventh Plan.

## OTHER ACTIVITIES OF CHILD WELFARE

### Cooperation with UNICEF

UNICEF projects are being implemented in India through Master Plan of Operations (MPO), which is an agreement prepared after mutual consultation and consensus within the framework of Basic Agreement signed between India and UNICEF in 1978. India is the largest Country Programme of UNICEF in the world.

The Programmes are being implemented through various Ministries and Departments dealing with children which includes Ministry of Women and Child Development, Department of Elementary Education and Literacy, Department of Family Welfare and NACO, Ministry of Social Justice and Empowerment, Ministry of Labour, Ministry of Information and Broadcasting, Ministry of Youth Affairs and Sports, and Department of Drinking Water Supply (Rajiv Gandhi National Drinking Water Mission).

The Ministry of Women Child Development is the nodal Ministry for coordinating the implementation of the Master Plan of Operations. The Ministry of Women and Child Development conducts periodic review meetings to coordinate and monitor the implementation and expenditure of the UNICEF programmes in India.

The total allocation for the last UNICEF-GOI Programme of Co-operation for the period 2003-2007 is US$ 400 million. An additional funds of US $ 100 million has also been approved by UNICEF for utilization in the current MPO period.

The current Master Plan of Operations for the period 2003-07 was signed by GOI & UNICEF on 13th January, 2003.

The MPO aims to achieve the following objectives: - (a) to empower families and communities with appropriate knowledge and skills to improve the care and protection of children (b) to expand partnerships as a way to leverage resources for children and scale up interventions (c) to strengthen the evaluation and knowledge base of best practices on children.

The programme contribute towards (a) reduction in infant and maternal mortality (b) improvements in levels of child nutrition (c) ensuring universal elementary education (d) enhancing child protection (e) protection of children and adolescents from HIV/AIDS.

The major activities included in different sectoral programmes are given below:

- Education
- Child Development and Nutrition

- Child Protection
- Reproductive and Child Health
- Child's Environment: Water, Environment and Sanitation
- HIV/AIDS
- Advocacy and Partnerships

India is annually contributing an amount of Rs. 3.80 crore to UNICEF

**Assistance to Voluntary Organisations for providing Social Defence Services**

Under the scheme, assistance is given to voluntary organisations working in the field of child and women welfare for innovative projects and activities which are not covered in the existing schemes of the Ministry of Women and Child Development. Under the Scheme in addition to the innovative projects being sanctioned in the field of women and child development projects are also sanctioned for combating trafficking in source areas and destination areas.

**National Awards: National Child Award for Exceptional Achievement**

The National Child Award for Exceptional Achievement was instituted in 1996 to give recognition to the children with exceptional abilities and who have achieved outstanding status in various fields including academics, arts, culture and sports etc. Children between the age of 4 to 15 years who have shown an exceptional achievement in any field including academics, arts, culture and sports, etc., are to be considered for this award. One Gold Medal and 35 silver Medals (one for each State/UT) are to be given annually.

The Awards for the child with exceptional achievement shall consists of :-

**(A) Gold Medal – 1 (One)**

i. A cash prize of Rs.20,000/-

ii. A Citation and certificates, and

iii. A Gold Medal

**(B) Silver Medals – 35 (Thirty five)**

i. Award money Rs.10,000/- for each awardee.

ii. A citation and certificate for each awardee, and

iii. A Silver Medal for each awardee.

## NATIONAL AWARD FOR CHILD WELFARE

The Award was instituted in 1979 to honour five institutions and three individuals for their outstanding performance in the field of child welfare. The National Award for Child Welfare includes a cash prize of Rs. 3 lakh and a certificate for each institution and Rs. 1 lakh and a certificate for each individual.

**Rajiv Gandhi Manav Seva Award**

This Award was instituted in 1994 to honour an individual who makes outstanding contribution towards service for children. The Award carries a cash prize of Rs. 1 lakh, a silver plaque and a citation.

**Parliamentary Forum on Children**

A Parliamentary Forum on Children under the Chairpersonship, Speaker Lok Sabha has been constituted to deal with all issues pertaining to children. The officers of the Ministry of Women and Child Development attend the meeting and note the suggestions made during the meeting.

**Working Group on Development of Children**

A Working Group on Development of Children under the Chairpersonship,Secretary, Ministry of Women and Child Development has been constituted by the Planning Commission for preparing the Eleventh Plan. The Working Group held its first meeting on 31st July, 2006 and decided to constitute four Sub Groups in the fields of ICDS and Nutrition, Early Childhood Education, Child Protection and Girl Child. The Sub Groups prepared their reports and submitted to the Working Group in the month of August 2006. The Working Group held its second meeting on 25th Aug., 2006 and constituted a Drafting Committee for putting together the reports of the Sub Groups and for preparing the final report of the Working Group. The final Report of the Working Group has been sent to the Planning Commission.

☆☆☆☆☆

6

CHAPTER

# MILESTONES IN CHILD RIGHTS - NATIONAL

**"There can be no keener revelation of a society's soul than the way in which it treats its children."**

— *Nelson Mandela*

We all know that India became independent on 15 August 1947. Independence ushered in a new era for children. The historical process, and its social, economic and political priorities from mid-nineteenth to mid-twentieth century, paved the way for shaping a more coherent concept of childhood located within the family as the principal institutional influence and as the prime site for socialization. Further, it determined the nature of the relationship between the child, the family and the State and thus, created the essential foundation of a national childhood for all children.

Correspondingly, the Constitution of India, which came into force in January 1950, contains provisions for survival, development and protection of children. These are included both in Part III and Part IV of the Constitution pertaining to 'Fundamental Rights' and 'Directive Principles of State Policy'. A list of major constitutional provisions relating to children is given below—

## FUNDAMENTAL RIGHTS

The Constitution of India recognizes the vulnerable position of children and their right to protection.

Following the doctrine of protective discrimination, it guarantees in Article 15 special attention to children through necessary and special laws and policies that safeguard their rights. The right to equality, protection of life and personal liberty and the right against exploitation are enshrined in Articles 14, 15, 15(3), 19(1) (a), 21, 21(A), 23, 24, and reiterate India's commitment to the protection, safety, security and well-being of all its people, including children.

**Article 14:**

The State shall not deny to any person equality before the law or the equal protection of the laws within the territory of India;

**Article 15:**

The State shall not discriminate against any citizen on grounds only of religion, race, caste, sex, place of birth or any of them;

**Article 15 (3):**

Nothing in this article shall prevent the State from making any special provision for women and children;

**Article 19(1)(a)**

All citizens shall have the right to freedom of speech and expression;

**Article 21:**

Protection of life and personal liberty — No person shall be deprived of his life or personal liberty except according to procedure established by law;

**Article 21A:**

Free and compulsory education for all children of the age of 6 to 14 years;

**Article 23:**

Prohibition of traffic in human beings and forced labour—(1) Traffic in human beings and beggars and other similar forms of forced labour are prohibited and any contravention of this provision shall be an offence punishable in accordance with law;

**Article 24:**

Prohibition of employment of children in factories, etc. No child below the age of fourteen years shall be employed to work in any factory or mine or engaged in any other hazardous employment;

## Directive Principles of State Policy

**Article 39:**

The state shall, in particular, direct its policy towards securing:

(e) that the health and strength of workers, men and women, and the tender age of children are not abused and that citizens are not forced by economic necessity to enter vocations unsuited to their age or strength;

(f) that children are given opportunities and facilities to develop in a healthy manner and in conditions of freedom.

**Article 45:**

The State shall endeavour to provide within a period of ten years from the commencement of this Constitution, for—free and compulsory education for all children until they complete the age of fourteen years.

**Article 46:**

To promote with special care the educational and economic interests of the weaker sections of the people, especially the Scheduled Castes and Scheduled Tribes,

**Article 47:**

The State shall regard the raising of the level of nutrition and the standard of living of its people and the improvement of public health as among its primary duties and, in particular, the State shall endeavour to bring about prohibition of the consumption except for medicinal purposes of intoxicating drinks and of drugs which are injurious to health.

Being one of the world's largest democracies, India has a federal system of government, with the States having their own democratically elected governments. The relative jurisdiction of the Central and State Governments over different matters has been indicated in the Seventh Schedule of the Constitution of India under the Union, State and Concurrent Lists. The survival, development and protection of children fall either in the Concurrent or in the State List. However, the implementation of schemes, including those of the Central Government, is carried out by the States. The 73$^{rd}$ and 74$^{th}$ Constitutional amendments have recognised a third tier, below that of the State Government, *viz.*, Panchayati Raj Institutions (PRIs), giveing them financial and administrative powers, and listed the subjects falling in their area of activities, a number of which relate to those services which have a direct bearing on children.

Development programmes in the country, including those for children, are carried out within the framework of the Five-Year Plans. Some of these programmes are wholly funded by the Central Government, some by both Central and State Governments, and some entirely by the State Government, depending on whether the programmes are classified as Central, centrally sponsored or State sector schemes. In addition, a wide variety of programmes are also being implemented in collaboration with international organisations and non-governmental organisations, which are now growing as a vibrant sector in the development and empowerment of children.

In the ensuing paragraphs, let us now see the milestones achieved by India on the whole ever since it achieved independence with regard to survival, development, protection and participation of children both at the national and international level.

The **First Five-Year Plan (1951-56)** took a comprehensive review of resources and needs of children along with women to meet the problems that had emanated out of the Second World War and the partition of the country. Health, nutrition and education of children were identified as special areas of concern. In order to focus attention on these areas, it was decided to forge a viable partnership with the voluntary sector. Correspondingly, in 1953, the Central

Social Welfare Board (CSWB) was constituted with the object especially of assisting voluntary agencies in organising welfare programmes for children, women and handicapped persons. The Board assisted 591 child welfare organisations during the First Five-Year Plan. Besides, in collaboration with State Governments, the Board set up State Welfare Boards throughout the country. In 1954, Welfare Extension Projects were started to reach children and women in rural areas through the creation of balwadis and mahila mandals. Special programmes were also taken up to meet the needs of delinquents, destitute, handicapped and other group of children. For this, extensive training was provided to childcare functionaries engaged in carrying out different kinds of programmes for children. In addition,the Government of India passed the Protection of Civil Rights Act, 1955 and ratified the International Labour Organization (ILO) Convention No. 5 of 1919 on minimum age of work in industry.

The **Second Five-Year Plan (1956-61)** aimed at stabilising the child welfare system. As such, the activities of CSWB were further strengthened. In 1956, the Suppression of Immoral Traffic in Women and Girls Act (SITA) was enacted in pursuance of Government of India's ratification of the United Nations Convention for the Suppression of the Traffic in Persons and the Exploitation of the Prostitution of Others in the year 1950. Some of the other legislations enacted in the year 1956 were the Hindu Adoption and Maintenance Act, Hindu Minority and Guardianship Act, Women's and Children's Institutions (Licensing) Act and Young Persons (Harmful Publications) Act. In 1957, the Welfare Extension Projects were reviewed. This led to the launching of Coordinated Welfare Extension Projects in 1958. The Central and State Governments also stepped in to share the responsibility of implementing the schemes and programmes for destitutes and delinquents under the Children's Act, 1960. Special programmes were also undertaken for education, training and rehabilitation of handicapped children. During the Plan period, existing health, nutrition and education services were further strengthened and expanded. In1957, the National Bravery Award Scheme was instituted and 14th November, which also happens to be the birthday of our first Prime Minister, Pt. Jawaharlal Nehru was declared as Universal Children's Day. However, much before the 1959 Declaration came into existence; Indian Constitution had reflected all these 10 principles including the articles contained in the UDHR. Nonetheless, the Government of India subscribed to the principles enshrined in the Declaration and ensured that adequate steps were taken to guarantee these rights to children.

It thus moved ahead with its **Third Five-Year Plan (1961-66)** with increased emphasis on intersectoral coordination of services for children. An attempt was simultaneously made to coordinate health, education and welfare services. The Third Plan also recognised that the child was a human being with special needs. A significant achievement was the establishment of the Department of Social Security in June 1964, so as to give concerted attention to the problems and needs of children. This Department was later renamed as the Department of Social Welfare in January 1966, and was finally elevated to the status of an independent Ministry of Social Welfare in August 1979. This Ministry is today known by the nomenclature of Social Justice and Empowerment. To counter poor levels of nutrition, Applied Nutrition Programme was introduced in 1963. Later, in the year 1965, Food and Nutrition Board was setup in the Department of Food. Recognising the need to rectify the existent imbalance of educational facilities at the primary, middle and high school levels and the fact that the State was unable to fulfil its constitutional obligation of providing free and compulsory education to all children within a period of ten years, the Third Plan setup an Education Commission under the chairmanship of Dr. D.S. Kothari to find out possible solutions. The recommendations of the Kothari Commission led to the formulation of the National Education Policy in 1968 which in a way gave fillip to the efforts being made in the education sector. A Committee on Child Care was also constituted whose recommendations gave way to a comprehensive Scheme of Family and Child Welfare in 1967, 'thereby' providing integrated services to pre-school children in villages and basic training to women in craft, health education, nutrition and child care.

The **Fourth Five-Year Plan (1969-74)** focussed on development of a package of basic minimum services for children. It also drew attention to the problems of neglected and destitute children and introduced a Scheme for Children in Need for Care and Protection. In 1974, the National Policy for Children was adopted. The Policy Resolution recognised children as the nation's supremely important asset and declared that it is the responsibility of the State to nurture them. It further emphasised that it shall be the duty of the State to "provide adequate services to children, both before and after birth and through the period of growth, to ensure their full physical, mental and social development." And that the "State shall progressively increase the scope of such services so that within a reasonable time, all children in the country enjoy optimum conditions for their balanced growth." To achieve these objectives, it called for the adoption of following measures – comprehensive health programme; provision of nutritional services; nutrition and nutrition education to expectant and nursing mothers; free and compulsory education to all children up to the age of 14 years; provision of non-formal education; promotion of physical education and other types of recreational as well as cultural and scientific activities in schools and community centres; provision of special assistance to children belonging to the weaker sections of society; upliftment of children in distress; protection against neglect, cruelty and exploitation of children; protection against child labour; provision of special facilities for children ailing from various kinds of disabilities and encouragement and assistance to gifted children especially those belonging to the weaker sections of the society. In achieving the above, the Policy gave special recognition to the role of voluntary organisations. Right to health being a basic human right, the Fourth Plan accorded high priority to Mother and Child Health Programme (MCH). The Special Nutrition Programme, Balwadi Nutrition Programme and Prophylaxis Scheme against Blindness due to Vitamin A Deficiency among Children were also introduced in 1970-71. The voluntary organisations too continued to work in partnership with the Government and some on their own.

The **Fifth Five-Year Plan (1974-79)** saw a shift in focus from child welfare to child development wherein emphasis was laid on further integration and coordination of services, increased allocations and introduction of new schemes for children. The adoption of National Policy for Children led to the constitution of the National Children's Board in December, 1974 under the presidentship of the Prime Minister for planning, reviewing and coordination of services and programmes to meet the needs of children. The scheme of Integrated Child Development Services (ICDS) was launched on 2 October 1975. Launching of the ICDS was a logical culmination of efforts pursued through the earlier four Five-Year Plans. In 1975, the Government ratified the ILO Convention No. 123 of 1965 relating to minimum age for underground work. The Minimum Needs Programme was also launched in order to enhance the capacity of families and communities. The ICDS scheme is considered to be one of the largest outreach programmes for children in the world. It presently covers almost all the development blocks in India. The scheme adopts a multi-sectoral approach to child well-being, incorporating health, education and nutrition interventions, and is implemented through a network of anganwadi centers (AWCs) at the community level. At these centers, anganwadi workers and their helpers provide eight key services to 0-6 year old children along with expectant and nursing mothers, covering supplementary nutrition, immunisation, health check-ups and referral services, health and nutrition education to adult women, micronutrient supplementation and pre-school education for 3 to 6 year old children. As the programme has developed over the years, it has expanded its range of interventions to include components focussed on adolescent girls' nutrition, health, awareness and skills development, as well as income generation schemes for women. The year 1979 holds great significance in the history of child welfare and development. Being designated as the International Year of the Child (IYC) by the United Nations General Assembly, number of activities and programmes were undertaken throughout the world in this year. In India, a National Plan of Action was prepared to observe the IYC. The main theme of the National Plan of Action was 'Reaching the Deprived Children'. Based on the model of National Plan of Action, many State Governments in India as well as non-governmental organisations formulated their own plans of action with specific programmes and activities to be taken up during the year in their respective areas. All this gave a great impetus to the on-going programmes related to children in India. The year also saw the United Nations Commission on Human Rights starting work on the drafting of the Convention on the Rights of the Child (CRC). The initiative to draft the Convention came from Poland and the Commission responded by setting-up a multi-country Working Group. In India, another important achievement during the year was settingup of the National Children's Fund to provide assistance to voluntary organisations. During IYC, the National Awards for Child Welfare was instituted. In the health sector, the Government of India signed the Alma Ata Declaration of 1978 and committed itself to the goal of 'Health for All by 2000 A.D'. The Expanded Programme of Immunisation was also introduced in 1978. In the area of nutrition, various nutrition intervention programmes being implemented were strengthened and expanded including the Prophylaxis against Iron and Vitamin A Deficiency Programmes. In 1975, the Scheme of Crèches/Day Care Centres for Children of Working and Ailing Mothers was launched by the CSWB. In 1976, the Child Marriage Restraint Act of 1929 was amended and in 1978, the SITA enacted in 1956 was modified. In 1976, the Bonded Labour (System) Abolition Act was enacted.

The **Sixth Five-Year Plan (1980-85)** reiterated the approach and strategy adopted for children during the Fifth Plan and further promoted integration and strengthening of child welfare and development programmes started earlier. During the International Year of Disabled in 1981 vigorous efforts were made to implement various education, training and rehabilitation programmes for the physically handicapped children. Preventive and development services of domiciliary nature were accorded priority over institutional care for destitutes, delinquents and handicapped children. The problem of working children and their welfare simultaneously received attention of the planners for the first time during the Sixth Five-Year Plan and appropriate programmes were undertaken to improve the health, nutrition and educational status of working children. In 1981, the Central Child Labour Advisory Board was setup to review implementation of existing laws concerning child labour. In 1982, the Scheme of Early Childhood Education was introduced as a strategy to reduce dropout rate and improve the rate of retention in schools. The Development of Women and Children in Rural Areas was another scheme that was introduced in the year 1982. Another important milestone in the Sixth Plan period was the formulation of the National Health Policy in the year 1983. The same year, the Government of India recognised the International Code on the Marketing of Breast Milk Substitutes that was adopted by the World Health Assembly and formulated the Indian National Code for Protection and Promotion of Breast Feeding. ICDS was used as a major nutrition intervention programme as well as a vehicle for promoting elementary education among children.

The **Seventh Five-Year Plan (1985-90)** led to spatial expansion and enrichment of child development services. In order to give focussed attention and direction to child development, a separate Department of Women and Child Development was setup for the first time in the Ministry of Human Resource Development in September 1985. Its status was elevated to that of an independent Ministry of Women and Child Development in 2006 and issues concerning children that were earlier being dealt by the Ministry of Social Justice and Empowerment have now been transferred to it. The ICDS continued to be the main integrated national programme for early childhood survival and development during the Seventh Plan period. To deal effectively with the problem of neglected children and children in conflict with law, the Juvenile Justice Act, 1986 was legislated, repealing the then Children's Act of 1960. To implement the provisions of the 1986 Act, a Scheme of Prevention and Control of Social Maladjustment was initiated in 1986-87. The Government also enacted the Child Labour (Prohibition and Regulation) Act, 1986. In 1987, the National Policy on Child Labour was announced. National Child Labour Projects were started in areas where there was high concentration of child labour. Simultaneously, efforts were made to expand crèche services for children of Central Adoption Resource Agency (CARA.) CARA grants recognition to Indian placement agencies on the recommendations of the State Government for processing inter-country adoption. It also accords enlistment to foreign agencies that are engaged in sponsoring applications of foreign prospective adoptive parents. These agencies are licensed by the appropriate Government Department in their country of origin to mediate in country and inter-country adoptions and their applications for enlistment/renewal are forwarded and recommended by India's Diplomatic Mission. The main thrust in the programmes for children who were handicapped was on prevention of disabilities and development of their functional skills. In 1985, the Scheme of District Rehabilitation Centres was introduced as a Pilot Project. In 1986, the Government further modified the SITA and also changed the name of the Act to Immoral Traffic (Prevention) Act to cover all persons, whether male or female, who were exploited sexually for commercial purposes. These apart, stringent punishments were prescribed for offences involving children. Another notable milestone of the Seventh Plan was setting up of a Central Adoption Resource Agency (CARA) in 1990 to deal with matters relating to adoption. Later, during the Eighth Five-Year Plan, the Government pioneered a Scheme of Assistance to Homes for Infants (Shishu Greh) to Promote In-country Adoption. Under the MCH programme, efforts were made to reduce Infant Mortality Rate (IMR) and Maternal Mortality Rate (MMR). In the year 1985, the Universal Immunisation Programme was launched under the MCH programme to protect children from six major diseases which affected early childhood mortality and morbidity, *viz.*, diptheria, whooping cough, tetanus, polio, measles and childhood tuberculosis. In 1986-87, emphasis was laid on Oral Rehydration Therapy Programme to prevent diarrhoeal deaths among children. The National Diarrhoeal Disease Control Programme was made part of the MCH Programme. In the education sector, the strategies of the Seventh Plan underwent a change in the middle of the Plan period with the adoption of a new National Policy on Education (NPE) in 1986. Taking a holistic view, the NPE visualised education as a dynamic, cumulative, life-long process, providing diversity of learning opportunities to all segments of society. Its main purpose was to fulfil the objective of "Education for All" by providing early childhood care and education, universalising elementary education through formal and non-formal methods, reducing wastage and involving the local community in the management of early education. As a result, new schemes were implemented like the District Primary Education Programme in 1986 and the Operation *Blackboard* in 1987. Besides, the Scheme of Non-formal Education was revised. Few of the other important initiatives taken by the Government in selected areas especially in educationally backward States, were the Shiksha Karmi Project and Lok Jumbish Project in Rajasthan, Bihar Education Project and the Andhra Pradesh Primary Education Project. The NPE in its own way tried to provide scope for equal access to education to all, irrespective of class, caste, creed or gender. In addition, it envisaged a common educational structure like 10+2+3 and common core curriculum throughout the country. It also sought to remove disparities by catering to the needs of Scheduled Castes, Scheduled Tribes, the handicapped and other minority groups. To look into the problems of street children, the Ministry of Social Justice and Empowerment introduced the Integrated Programme for Street Children.

At the regional level, India actively promoted and supported the 1986 decision of South Asian Association for Regional Cooperation (SAARC) to take up the issue of children as a summit concern, and to declare first a year and then a decade for the girl child (1990-2000). At the international level, the Convention on the Rights of the Child (CRC) was approved by the General Assembly of the United Nations on 20th November 1989 (the thirtieth anniversary of the adoption of the Declaration of the Rights of the Child). This Convention was formally opened for signature and ratification on 26th January 1990, and various nations vied to be the first to sign and ratify, a race that was won by Ghana when the Secretary General of the United Nations received that country's instrument of ratification on 5th February 1990. Previous United Nations human rights treaties had taken several years to receive the minimum number of ratifications necessary for their entry into force.

The focus in the **Eighth Five-Year Plan (1992-97)** was on human development through advocacy, mobilisation and community empowerment and it accorded high priority to survival and development of children. The ICDS continued to be the basic strategy for child survival and development focussing on areas predominantly inhabited by the tribal people, Scheduled

Castes as well as drought-prone regions and urban slums. In fact, the scheme of ICDS was universalised covering all the Community Development Blocks and major slums in the country. As has been pointed out earlier, the Government of India ratified the CRC in the year 1992. This provided a strong base for initiating necessary legal and other developmental measures for protecting and promoting the rights of children in consonance with the CRC. During 1993-94, the National Crèche Fund (NCF) was set-up to meet the growing demand for crèches. The NCF extended financial assistance for the opening of crèches besides conversion of the existing Anganwadis-cum-Crèches. Concerted efforts were simultaneously made to tackle the problem of social deviance, juvenile delinquency and juvenile crime through preventive, correctional and rehabilitative services. On 15th August 1994, a programme to Eliminate Child Labour in Hazardous Employment by 2000 was announced. Prior to this, in Government of India joined the International Programme on Elimination of Child Labour launched by ILO. Subsequently, the National Authority for Elimination of Child Labour was constituted on 26th September 1994 to lay down policies and programmes for elimination of child labour. The enforcement of Child Labour (Prohibition and Regulation) Act, 1986 was also strengthened. In pursuance of the National Policy on Child Labour, specific projects were undertaken in industries where the incidents of child labour were found to be very high. Measures were taken to cover families of child labourers under income generation schemes. Public opinion on the evils of child labour was mobilised through investigative journalism, use of electronic media and the support of activists' groups. In the "Health for All" strategy, health for underprivileged including children was promoted consistently. The Child Survival and Safe Motherhood (CSSM) programme was launched during the year 1992-93 to strengthen MCH services. Other measures promoted were: greater access for mothers to pre-natal care; training of midwives so that a larger percentage of births took place with the aid of trained attendants; and spreading of awareness in families about the special health and nutrition needs of pregnant women. With a view to regulate and prevent the misuse of modern pre-natal diagnostic techniques, particularly abortion of female foetuses, Pre-natal Diagnostic Techniques (Regulation and Prevention of Misuse) Act,1994 was introduced. Prior to this, the Infant Milk Substitutes, Feeding Bottles and Infant Foods (Regulation and Production, Supply and Distribution), Act was formulated in 1992. This came into force on 1th August 1993. During the Eighth Five-Year Plan, the National AIDS Control Organisation was established under the Ministry of Health and Family Welfare to strengthen the management capacity for prevention and control of HIV/AIDS. In the year 1993, the National Nutrition Policy was adopted to combat the problem of malnutrition. The Pulse Polio Immunisation Programme was also started in the year 1995. In the education sector, the main strategy for achieving the target of "Education for All by 2000 A.D." was adoption of a decentralised approach to planning. In pursuance of the revised National Policy on Education, 1992 and the Programme of Action, various steps were taken to expand early childhood care and education activities, and universalise elementary education. An NGO Cell was specifically set-up in 1994 to facilitate networking with NGOs on varied issues concerning children. In the year 1994, District Primary Education Programme (DPEP) was launched as a centrally sponsored scheme in 42 districts of seven States, with the aim of revitalizing and strengthening the existing system, tackling problem areas, developing innovative approaches with the district as a unit of planning. In adopting a holistic approach, emphasis was laid on converting existent programmes and services, and encouraging community participation.

The Eighth Plan specifically recognised the 'Girl Child' as an important target group, demanding attention of the Government for her development and to fight against the prevailing gender discrimination. The Eighth Plan marked the adoption of two National Plans of Action in 1992 – one for children and the other exclusively for the girl child. These Plans of Action committed themselves to achieve the goals pronounced in the 1990 World Summit on Survival, Protection and Development of Children. In conformity with these National Plans, many States prepared their own State Plan of Action for Children/for the Girl Child. Two separate Inter-Departmental Coordination Committees reviewed the progress of the implementation of these two Plans of Action at regular intervals. A few States also embarked upon specific schemes to improve the plight of the girl child. For example, Haryana instituted the 'Apni Beti Apna Dhan' Scheme, Tamil Nadu initiated the 'Cradle Scheme', Rajasthan introduced the 'Raj Lakshmi Scheme' and Madhya Pradesh the 'Bhagyalakshmi Scheme'. Another very important Act enacted by the Government of India in this Plan period was the Persons with Disabilities (Equal Opportunities, Protection of Rights and Full Participation) Act,1995 that came into force in February 1996. This law is an important landmark and is a significant step in the direction of ensuring equal opportunities for people with disabilities and their full participation in the nationbuilding.

At the international front, the World Conference on Human Rights was held in Vienna in the year 1993. The Vienna Declaration and Programme of Action urged States to ratify and implement promptly the CRC and the CEDAW. Taking a cue from all these developments, the Government of India submitted India's Initial State Party Report on CRC to the Committee on the Rights of the Child in March 1997. This Report was due for submission in 1995. In the year 1995, however, a four Member team of the CRC Committee visited India in October to make on the spot assessment about the specific problems of children in India. The CRC Committee as mentioned above, is made up of ten independent experts. Governments that ratify the Convention must report to the Committee, first within two years of ratification, and then every five-year. The Committee has circulated detailed guidelines to States, Parties as to what their reports should cover as the process of reporting involves a rigorous review of actions taken by them. It encourages "popular participation and public scrutiny of Government policies", which goes on to show that States, Parties are publicly and internationally accountable for the treatment meted out to their children. Another important milestone of the Eighth Five-Year Plan was that during the 1995 Beijing World Conference on Women, India was successful in convincing others to have a separate section on the girl child incorporated in the Beijing Platform for Action for the Advancement of Women.

In the **Ninth Five-Year Plan (1997-2002),** efforts were made to expedite effective implementation and achievement of the goals set in the two Plans of Action besides instituting a National Charter for Children to ensure that no child remains illiterate, hungry or lacks medical care. To ensure the 'survival, protection and development' of children, especially that of the girl child, the Ninth Plan concentrated on arresting the problem of declining sex-ratio as well as its other related problems of female foeticide and infanticide. These problems were attacked through a two-pronged strategy of both direct and indirect measures. While the direct measures included effective implementation of the existing legislation, the indirect measures were directed to change the mindset of the people in favour of the girl child, besides empowering women to exercise their reproductive rights and choices. In this endeavour, UNICEF made special efforts to launch a 10-year old cartoon character named Meena along with her pet parrot Mithu and brother Raju. The Meena Initiative, popular till date with both adults and children, uses the CRC and the CEDAW as tools with which to advocate for the rights of the girl child in South Asia. Meena makes a claim for the rights of all children and highlights the duties of families and obligations of States to realize those rights. Meena's questioning and reasoning seeks to enable families and communities to come up with positive solutions to deep-rooted discrimination, answers that are realistic and culturally sensitive. Special efforts were made to ensure effective enforcement of the Pre-natal Diagnostic Techniques (Regulation and Prevention of Misuse) Act, 1994. In order to fulfil the birth right of every child to 'development', especially of those belonging to the disadvantaged and deprived groups as well as those with special needs, the Ninth Plan continued to focus on three major areas of child development, *viz.*, health, nutrition and education. In the field of 'Health', the scope of the erstwhile programme of CSSM was further widened into a comprehensive programme of 'Reproductive and Child Health' (RCH) that laid special emphasis on child survival and other related measures. Continued emphasis was laid on the ICDS. Under the Universal Immunisation Programme, significant achievements were made to arrest the problem of diphtheria, pertussis, neonatal tetanus, tuberculosis, poliomyelitis and measles. The special drive of Pulse Polio launched during 1995-96 was continued to eliminate the problem of poliomyelitis. All this had a definite impact in reducing the Infant Mortality Rate. The Government of India also committed to provide safe drinking water and sanitation facilities to every village to achieve the goal of 'Health for All'. In the field of 'Nutrition', children below the age of 6 years along with expectant and nursing mothers, received highest priority in line with the provisions of the National Nutrition Policy, 1993 and the National Plan of Action on Nutrition, 1995. Despite the shortfalls that were recorded in terms of feeding and funding by the State Governments, the coverage under Special Nutrition Programme reached 31.5 million children in the age group of 0-6 years. Similarly, the coverage under the National Programme of Nutritional Support to Primary Education commonly known as Mid-day Meals reached 105 million school children in the age group of 6-14 years by the end of the Ninth Plan.

In the field of 'Education', in consonance with the National Policy on Education as revised in 1992 and the Programme of Action, special thrust was given to the measures of Universal Primary Education. As a result of this, the country made impressive achievements whereby the number of schools increased four-fold from 2.31 lakh in 1950-51 to 9.88 lakh in 1999-2000, while the enrolment at the primary level jumped up by about six times from 19.2 million to 113.6 million. In 2001-02, the Sarva Shiksha Abhiyan (SSA) was launched with the aim of providing quality elementary education to all children in the 6-14 age group by 2010, besides bridging all gender and social category gaps at primary stage by 2007.

Concerted efforts were made to eliminate all forms of discrimination and violations against the rights of the girl child. The Ninth Plan also provided special incentives to the mother and the girl child so that the birth of a girl child in a family was rejoiced. To this effect, in the year 1997, Balika Samriddhi Yojana (BSY) was launched whereby a special package consisting of Rs.500/- to the mother and annual scholarship ranging from Rs.300/- to Rs.1,000/- for education of girl children from class 1 to 10 was provided to all those families living below the poverty line to ensure that all girl children went to schools. The incentive of Rs.500/- to the mother on the delivery of a girl child was limited to two girl children only. Similar initiatives were also launched by other State Governments. In 1999, the BSY was reviewed and recast to make it more effective. In 1998, the Government with the support of UNICEF launched a special service for children called Childline. This is a free phone service that can be accessed by a child or anyone on his/her behalf simply by dialling the number 1098. At present, Childline is working in 68 cities through a network of NGOs which not only responds to the needs of children but also plays a major role in crises intervention, long term care and rehabilitation. Realizing the need for an effective service delivery to children in need of care and protection, a National Initiative for Child Protection was launched through the National Institute of Social Defence and Childline India Foundation. It aimed at building partnerships with the State Departments of Social/Child Welfare, Childline Service and allied systems for protection and promotion of children's rights. In 1998, the Government of India instituted a Plan of Action to Combat Trafficking and Commercial Sexual Exploitation of Women and Children. Strong regulatory and administrative measures were taken to prevent exploitation of child labour. A thorough review of the Juvenile Justice Act, 1986 was undertaken whereby the Act was repealed by the Juvenile Justice (Care and Protection of Children) Act,2000. Likewise, a review of major existing child-specific and child related legislations was also undertaken to plug the loopholes in their implementation, *viz.*, the Child Marriage Restraint Act, 1929; the Immoral Traffic (Prevention) Act, 1956; the Child Labour (Prohibition and Regulation) Act, 1986; and the Pre-Natal Diagnostic Techniques (Regulation and Prevention of Misuse) Act, 1994. As per the commitment made by the Government of India to the CRC Committee, a Bill for setting up of a National Commission for Children to safeguard their rights was drafted in 2001. Prior to this, a Special Expert Committee chaired by Justice Shri V.R. Krishna Iyer prepared a Children's Code Bill 2000. The UNICEF India Country Office facilitated this entire exercise. But this venture proved to be futile as the Ministry of Women and Child Development felt that it was an independent exercise where the Government was not consulted at all. The 2001 draft Bill 'thus' never saw the light of the day. Efforts were concurrently made to develop a national level 'Information Network System' for women and children with emphasis on collection of gender-specific data with the objective of preparing a Gender Development Index so as to assess the socio-economic status of women and children on a continuing basis. A scheme entitled Kishori Shakti Yojana (KSY) was introduced as an enriched version of the Scheme for Adolescent Girls that was being implemented as part of the ICDS, to improve the nutritional and health status of girls in the age group of 11-18 years as well as equip them with vocational skills so that they could be gainfully engaged. In January 2000, the CRC Committee reviewed the Initial State Party Report that had been submitted by the Government of India and gave its Concluding Observations and Recommendations. India's First Periodic Report (Second Report) on CRC Implementation was due for submission in 2000.

However, the Government of India could only submit the Report in 2001. The 2001 Report made all out efforts to address the Observations and Recommendations that were given by the CRC Committee in connection with India's Initial Report. The CRC Committee at its 932nd & 933rd meeting held on 21th January 2004 considered India's First Periodic Report and gave its Concluding Observations and also recommended that India should submit its next Periodic Report by 10th July 2008.

In the **Tenth Five-Year Plan (2002 – 2007),** overall emphasis has been on a rights-based approach with regard to 'survival, development and protection' of children. Accordingly, focussed attention is being given to arrest the problem of declining sex ratio including its offshoots – female foeticide and female infanticide. Special efforts are being made to ensure effective enforcement of related legislations to prevent and eradicate the problem of female foeticide and female infanticide. In this context, in the year 2003, the Pre-natal Diagnostic Techniques (Regulation and Prevention of Misuse) Act, 1994 was amended. The amended Act is now called the Pre-Conception & Pre-Natal Diagnostic Techniques (Prohibition of Sex Selection) Act. Emphasis is simultaneously being laid on compulsory registration of births and deaths, as visualised in the National Population Policy (NPP) 2000.

To ensure 'development' of children, especially those belonging to the disadvantaged and deprived groups, focussed attention is being given once again on three core sectors, *viz.*, health, nutrition and education. All out efforts are being made to improve the coverage levels in respect of the six vaccine preventable diseases. Special efforts are being made to improve the coverage levels through the Universal Immunisation Programme which is being implemented as part of the RCH programme. Attempts, in particular, are being made to assess the health needs of all children at PHC level so as to undertake area-specific micro planning whereby all their needs are met through high quality RCH services. Further, it is being ensured that the Child Survival Programme of RCH will entail universal screening of all pregnant women so as to identify and manage those at high risk from the point of view of bringing about reduction in the pre-natal and neo-natal mortality and morbidity. In addition, the NPP and the revised National Health Policy,2002 are expected to extend both policy and programmatic support with definite targets to ensure child survival.

Along with the above, the two on-going direct feeding programmes of Special Nutrition as part of the ICDS and the National Programme for Nutrition Support to Primary Education have been streamlined and strengthened. Moreover, as a follow-up of the announcement made by the Prime Minister in his Independence Day Speech of 2001, a National Nutrition Mission was set-up in 2002 with an overall responsibility of reducing/eliminating both macro and micro nutritional deficiencies in the country. The overall approach adopted for the holistic development of children through the ICDS has since continued along with the on-going scheme for the Adolescent Girls, *viz.*, KSY. Recognising the increasing need for support services of crèches/day care centres for the children of working/ ailing mothers, especially in the present day context where more and more women are coming out for employment both in the organised and unorganised sectors, the NCF has been further strengthened to provide a wide network of crèches all over the country.

With regard to education, the Constitution (86th Amendment) Act was notified in December 2002, making free and compulsory education a Fundamental Right for all children in the age group of 6-14 years. The fact that Article 21A was added to the Constitution for recognising right to primary education implies that right to personal liberty guaranteed by Article 21 is now also the basis for a general right to education. Correspondingly, Article 45 of the Constitution has been substituted so as to provide for early childhood care and education for all children till they complete the age of 6 years. Article 51A was further modified by adding a clause – (k) – stating that it is the duty of the parents/guardians to provide opportunities for education to their children/ward between the age of six and fourteen years. Ever since education became a Fundamental Right, the Tenth Plan adopted a new approach towards achieving the goal of Universalisation of Elementary Education (UEE). As pointed out earlier since most of the programmes in the field of elementary education were disjointed in nature, Sarva Shiksha Abhiyan was launched in 2001-02 for providing comprehensive elementary education to all children. The SSA is seen as a major vehicle for achieving the goals of UEE in the Tenth Plan period. SSA is expected to solve the present problems of low rates of enrolment and retention, besides high dropout rates, especially amongst the girl children belonging to the Scheduled Castes, Scheduled Tribes, Other Backward Classes and Minorities. Through this programme, the Government aims to cover children who have never enrolled or those who have droppedout without completing eight years of elementary schooling. In terms of pre-school education, the Early Child Care Education component of ICDS continues to be a significant input for providing a soundfoundation for development as well as the first step in the education ladder.

Focussed attention is now being given to strengthening the early joyful period of play and learning in the young child's life to ensure a harmonious transition from the family environment to the primary school. In its quest to guarantee quality basic education throughout the country, the Government of India, in the year 2004, imposed an Education Cess @ 2 per cent on direct and indirect Central Taxes. At the international level, it adopted the Dakar Framework for Action on Education for All. The Framework identifies six goals, which includes, *inter alia*, progressive expansion of Early Childhood Care and Education, Universalization of Elementary Education by 2015, achieving Gender Equality in Education by 2015, and improvement in the quality of education.

Another very prominent legislation passed in the interest of children during the Tenth Five-Year Plan was the Goa Children's Act, 2003. The Act ensures protection for children and the young against exploitation of all kinds and against moral and material abandonment. In 2003, the Government of India ratified the 1993 Convention for the Protection of Children and Cooperation for Inter-country Adoption (The Hague Convention). The Juvenile Justice Act of 2000 was also modified. This Act is now known as the Juvenile Justice (Care and Protection of Children) Amendment Act, 2006. The year 2006 has been especially significant as the Commission for Protection of Child Rights Bill, 2005 was passed by the Parliament though the Child Rights Commission is yet to be set up. This is a big achievement not only for the children of the country but also for the Government for it was able to fulfil its commitment made to the CRC Committee for settingup a Child Rights Commission. The children and the people of the country would now have to wait and see how this Commission really functions. At the international level, the UN General Assembly's Special Session on Children was held in May 2002. It attracted 69 Summit-level participants and 190 high level national delegations apart from delegates representing NGOs from countries all over the world. It was for the first time in the history of UN meetings that more than 400 children participated as delegates. This Special Session dealt at length with the Millennium Development Goals and set forward quantitative and qualitative goals for children to be achieved by all United Nations Member States by the year 2015. Having accepted the Millennium Summit Declaration of 2000 and in order to achieve the targets set by the UN General Assembly, the Ministry of Women and Child Development subsequently drew up a fresh National Plan of Action for Children in the year 2005 with a hope that it would provide a roadmap for steps to be taken for bringing about improvement in the lives of Indian children.

The year 2005 was noteworthy as the Government of India ratified the two Optional Protocols to the CRC, *viz*., the Optional Protocol to the Convention on the Rights of the Child on the Sale of Children, Child Prostitution and Child Pornography and the Optional Protocol to the Convention on the Rights of the Child on the Involvement of Children in Armed Conflict. The UN General Assembly on 25$^{th}$ May 2000 had adopted both these Protocols. The former came into force on 18$^{th}$ January 2002 while the latter on 12$^{th}$ February 2002. It would be worthwhile to mention here that in the year 2002 the Government of India also signed the Protocol to Prevent,Suppress and Punish Trafficking in Persons, Especially Women and Children supplementing the United Nations Convention against Transnational Organized Crime, 2000. In addition to this, in 2002, the Government of India endorsed the SAARC Convention on Preventing and Combating Trafficking in Women and Children for Prostitution and the SAARC Convention on Regional Arrangements for the Promotion of Child Welfare in South Asia.

In 2006, the Committee on the Rights of the Child issued General Comments No. 8 and 9 relating to the Right of the Child to Protection from Corporal Punishment and Other Cruel or Degrading Forms of Punishment and the Rights of Children with Disabilities. Prior to this, in the year 2005, it had issued General Comments No. 6 and 7 pertaining to Treatment of Unaccompanied and Separated Children Outside their Country of Origin and Implementing Child Rights in Early Childhood. In the year 2003, the Committee had issued General Comments No. 3,4 and 5 relating to HIV/AIDS and the Rights of the Child, Adolescent Health and Development in the Context of the CRC and General Measures of Implementation of the Convention on the Rights of the Child. Before this, in the year 2002, it had issued General Comment No. 2 on the subject of the Role of Independent Human Rights Institutions. General Comment No. 1 was issued in the year 2001 that deals with the Aims of Education.

From the Seventh Five-Year Plan onwards, the judiciary and the Supreme Court too have played an active role in upholding the rights of the child. The Supreme Court of India has developed the concept of jurisdiction under which any individual can approach the Court with regard to the violation of a fundamental right. The Supreme Court has also modified traditional concepts by allowing groups of persons or organizations to intervene in cases relating to violations of fundamental rights even though they may not have been affected personally in the matter.

This concept of 'social action litigation' in India represents an effort to use the legal system to ensure action to realize constitutionally guaranteed rights.

The Draft Approach Paper of the **Eleventh Plan (2007-2012)** prepared by the Planning Commission, emphatically states that ***'Development of the child is at the centre of the EleventhPlan'.*** The first frame of reference for formulating the approach and commitments for children during the Eleventh Plan period is provided in the National Plan of Action for Children (NPAC) adopted by the Government of India in 2005, which has Cabinet approval. Time targets in the NPAC extend to 2012, the end-year of the Eleventh Plan. The NPAC sets out a range of positive measures and declares its intent to secure them for all children aged up to 18 years. It identifies the Constitution and the CRC as the guiding framework for realizing the rights of children below 18 years. It clearly implies cross-sectoral thinking and planning, and inter-sectoral measures. It also recognizes the importance of Panchayati Raj Institutions in reaching the development and protection goals and commitments towards children. The NPAC has identified twelve key priority areas for the utmost and sustained attention in terms of outreach, programme interventions and resource allocations. These are:

- Reducing **Infant Mortality Rate**
- Reducing **Maternal Mortality Rate**
- Reducing **Malnutrition** among children
- Achieving 100% civil **registration of births.**
- **Universalization of early childhood care and development and quality education for all children** achieving 100% access and retention in schools, including pre-schools.
- Complete **abolition of female foeticide, female infanticide and child marriage** and ensuring the survival, development and protection of the **girl child.**
- Improving **Water** and **Sanitation** coverage both in rural and urban areas
- Addressing and upholding the rights of **Children in Difficult Circumstances**.
- Securing for all children all legal and **social protection** from all kinds of abuse, exploitation and neglect
- Complete abolition of **child labour** with the aim of progressively eliminating all forms of economic exploitation of children.
- **Monitoring, Review, and Reform** of policies programmes and laws to ensure protection of children's interests and rights.
- Ensuring **child participation** and choice in matters and decisions affecting their lives
- The NPAC 2005 has articulated clearly the rights perspective and agenda for the development of children, and provides a robust framework within which to promote the survival, development, protection and participation of children. It is therefore logical and imperative that the NPAC 2005 becomes the basis for planning for children in the Eleventh Plan in all sectors and the principles articulated in it guide the planning and investments for children.

**The Guiding Principles of the NPAC are:**

- To regard the child as an asset and a person with human rights
- To address issues of discrimination emanating from biases of gender, class, caste, race, religion and legal status in order to ensure equality
- To accord utmost priority to the most disadvantaged, poorest of the poor and the least served child in all policy and programme interventions
- To recognize the diverse stages and settings of childhood, and address the needs of each, providing all children the entitlements that fulfill their rights and meet their needs in each situation.

Since the finalization of the NPAC 2005 the issues of children affected by HIV/AIDS and urban children in distress/difficult circumstances have also been accepted as key priorities by MWCD and will find a place in the Eleventh Plan as key priorities that need to be addressed.

The Draft Approach paper and the National Plan of Action for Children, 2005 have both identified the girl child as a special priority. The Eleventh Plan is to holistically empower the girl child in all aspects so that she can become an equal partner with boys on the road to development and progress. This requires addressing the various constraints /persisting problems facing the girl child. Towards this end, the strategy and action laid out in the National Plan of Action for Children and rights of the child will be given priority attention in all measures undertaken for girl children during the Plan.

In addition to the overall policy and commitment framework which will guide the development of the Eleventh Plan, it is important to keep in mind a holistic and rights based approach to child development, examine macro-perspective trends and trends in achievement of key national goals, and governance issues in order to evolve the specific approach and strategies for the Eleventh Plan on Child Rights and Development.Capacity building programmes for different functionaries and stake holders like law enforcement agencies, judiciary, parliamentarians, PRIs etc.

In accomplishing the milestones, the non-governmental and civil society organizations have played an equally important role along with the Government in virtually every aspect concerning children. The media too has played a critical role in shaping public opinion and creating mass awareness. The Government of India and UNICEF collaborative initiatives over the years have focussed on enhancing the capacities of the electronic and print media personnel in the Ministry of Information and Broadcasting so as to integrate and represent issues concerning children and their rights effectively. As a result, the media is gradually focussing on children's issues in a qualitative way. This is certainly a positive sign for the future and it is hoped that the media will increase its responsibility to include monitoring of child rights violations in a significant and persistent manner. It would be seen from this chapter that India has come a long way from 1947 to 2006 in achieving the milestones at the national and international level. All these efforts bear testimony to the overall concern of the Government and other stakeholders in reaching out to its children which are considered to be the supreme wealth of the nation. India is a home to more than 400 million children who are below the age of 18 years. While dealing with the complex dimensions of child rights, both in terms of numbers and in quality, we do feel satisfied about our country's progress in several fronts such as immunization and enhancement of literacy rates in recent years. At the same time, we are aware and deeply concerned about certain other critical indicators such as infant mortality, malnutrition and regional disparities. Our efforts should therefore be directed towards overcoming obstacles in these areas. Children in India represent diverse cultures, religions, castes, communities and economic groups.

The development of this human resource should be considered as a key national concern not only by the Government but also by all stakeholders. It is the prime responsibility of all concerned to ensure that proper foundation is laid in the early stages of children's life, so that their potential is properly harnessed for the growth and development of the nation. The Government, of course, is committed to do its best. However, despite its best efforts, there are children who suffer from hunger, diseases and discriminations of varied kinds. Not only this, they are subjected to exploitation and atrocities of all kinds.

☆☆☆☆☆

# 7 CHAPTER

# EDUCATION FOR CHILD RIGHTS — METHODS AND TECHNIQUES

**"Children are our most valuable natural resource."** —***Herbert Hoover***

The teacher will always be the key person, however, in getting new initiatives to work. The teacher therefore carries a great responsibility for communication of the child rights message. Opportunities to do this may vary: child rights themes may be infused into existing school subjects, such as history, civics, literature, art, geography, languages and scientific subjects, or may have a specific course allocated to them; human rights education may also be pursued through less formal education arenas within and outside schools such as after-school activities, clubs and youth forums.

Ideally, a child rights culture should be built into the whole curriculum (yet in practice, particularly at secondary level, it is usually treated piecemeal, as part of the established curriculum in the social and economic sciences and the humanities). In the classroom, child rights education should be developed with due attention to the developmental stage of children and their social and cultural contexts in order to make child rights principles meaningful to them. For example, child rights education for younger children could emphasize the development of self-esteem and empathy and a classroom culture supportive of child rights principles. Although young children are able to grasp the underlying principles of basic human rights instruments, the more complex content of human rights documents may be more appropriate to older learners with better developed capacities for concept development and analytical reasoning.

The focus of child rights education is not just outward on external issues and events but also inward on personal values, attitudes and behaviour. To affect behaviour and inspire a sense of responsibility for child rights education uses participatory methodologies that emphasize independent research, analysis and critical thinking.

## TEACHING ABOUT AND FOR HUMAN RIGHTS

The "child rights climate" within schools and classrooms should rest on reciprocal respect between all the actors involved. Accordingly, the way in which decisionmaking processes take place, methods for resolving conflicts and administering discipline, and the relationship within and among all actors constitute key contributing factors. Ultimately teachers need to explore ways to involve not only students, school administrators, education authorities and parents in child rights education but also the whole community. In this way teaching for child rights can reach from the classroom into the community to the benefit of both. All concerned will be able to discuss universal values and their relation to reality and to recognize that schools can be part of the solution to basic child rights problems.

## TEACHING AND PREACHING: ACTION SPEAKS LOUDER THAN WORDS

The fact that Convention on the Rights of the Child have virtual global validity and applicability is very important for teachers. For learning to have practical benefit, students need not only learn about child rights but to learn in an environment that models them. This means avoiding any hypocrisy. At its simplest, hypocrisy refers to situations where what a teacher is teaching is clearly at odds with how he or she is teaching it. For example: "Today we are going to talk about freedom of expression – shut up in the back row!" In such circumstances, students will learn mostly about power, and considerably less about child rights. As students spend a good deal of time studying teachers and can develop a good understanding of teachers' beliefs, a teacher who behaves unjustly or abusively will have little positive effect.

Sometimes controversial and sensitive subjects come up when students begin to examine child rights. Teachers need to remain constantly alert to student discomfort and potential disagreement. Teachers should acknowledge that child rights necessarily involve conflicts of values and that students will benefit from understanding these conflicts and seeking to resolve them. Sometimes teachers meet resistance to child rights education on the ground that it imposes non-native principles that contradict and threaten local values and customs. Teachers concerned about resistance from administrators should meet with them in advance, share goals and plans for the class, and explain about the United Nations human rights framework and related educational initiatives (such as the United Nations Decade for Human Rights Education). (Encourage administrators to visit a class – they may themselves benefit from human rights education move one place to the right and discuss the same topic with a new person). Personal or emotional topics are best discussed in pairs or small groups.

## PEDAGOGICAL TECHNIQUES FOR CHILD RIGHTS EDUCATION

These techniques have proved especially appropriate for child rights education because they encourage critical thinking, both cognitive and affective learning, respect for differences of experience and opinion, and active engagement of all participants in ongoing learning.

### Factors Affecting Selection of Strategies

1. The learner: Needs, interests, ability, knowledge base, age, achievement level, aptitudes, learning style, motivational values, developmental level, strengths and weaknesses, cultural and community background affect the learner.

2. The instructional objectives : Knowledge, skill, value objectives as well as social participation are considered in the instructional objectives.
3. The curriculum content : Some content is more effectively learned with a particular strategy. Content emphasis, adaptability, flexibility, objectives, content fairness, and format are other factors.
4. The number of participants : Direct teaching strategies involve large groups, and cooperative learning strategies involve small groups.
5. The classroom environment : Size, physical arrangement, décor, flexibility, portability, availability of open space, lighting affect teaching strategies.
6. Availability of time: Some may require more time than others.
7. The nature of strategy: Different strategies have different purposes, characteristics, advantages and limitations.
8. Teacher competencies: The teacher's competencies, knowledge of the strategy and experience with it could also be determing factors.
9. Availability of materials : Resources, equipment and other instructional materials are essential for the successful delivery of certain strategies to accomplish certain objectives.

### 1. Brainstorming

This technique can be used to seek solutions to problems that are both theoretical and practical. It requires a problem to be analyzed and then solutions to be developed. Brainstorming encourages a high degree of participation, and it stimulates those involved to maximum creativity.

Following presentation of a problem, all ideas in response to it are recorded on a board or chart paper. All responses are recorded; no explanations are required and no suggestions are judged or rejected at this stage. The teacher then categorizes and analyses the responses, at which stage some are combined, adapted or rejected. Finally the group makes recommendations and takes decisions on the problem.

### 2. Case Studies

Students in small groups work with real or fictional cases that require them to apply child rights standards. Case studies should be based on credible and realistic scenarios that focus on two or three main issues that can be presented to students for consideration in its entirety or "fed" to them sequentially as a developing situation (the "evolving hypothetical") to which they must respond. This method encourages analysis, problem-solving and planning skills, as well as cooperation and team building. Case studies can be used to set up debates, discussion or further research.

### 3. The Talking Circle

To engage the whole class in a topic, the teacher might use techniques like a "*Talk Around*" (i.e., the teacher asks an open-ended question like "What does dignity mean to you?" or "I feel happy when ..." and each student responds in turn).

A lively method of representing discussion graphically is the "*Discussion Web*". Students sit in a discussion circle and speak one at a time. As they do, they pass a ball of yarn along, letting it unwind in the process. Each person keeps hold of the string whenever it passes through her or his hands. Eventually the group is linked by a web of string, clearly showing the pattern of communication that has gone on within it.

### 4. Field trips/Community visits

Students benefit from the extension of school into the community,learning from places where child rights issues develop (e.g., courts, prisons, international borders) or where people work to defend rights or relieve victims (e.g., nonprofit organizations, food or clothing banks, free clinics).

The purpose of the visit should be explained in advance, and students should be instructed to pay critical attention and to record their observations for a subsequent discussion or written reflection following the visit.

### 5. Interviews

Interviews provide direct learning and personalize issues and history. Those interviewed might be family and community members, activists, leaders or eye-witnesses to child rights events. Such oral histories can contribute to documenting and understanding human right issues in the home community.

### 6. Socratic Questioning

Socrates believed that all people possess knowledge within themselves and the major role of the teacher is to help students bring forth this knowledge rather than to pass the teacher's knowledge on to their students. The Socratic method involves a strategy consisting of four parts:

a. A student states an initial proposition;

b. The teacher leads the student to doubt;

c. The teacher gets the student to admit that he does not know the way out of perplexity, and

d. The teacher guides the student in the pursuit of truth about the issue.

This method involves that perplexity serves as the motivation for further inquiry. Students clarify their thoughts by testing them against alternatives. It is an effective teaching strategy to use to demonstrate inconsistencies. It can be well used to illustrate to students that their opinions have contradicted a child rights principle that has already been agreed upon. Some student may argue that girls should not be included in the soccer team. But these same students may agree on equality of sexes. By using Socratic method the students are forced to evaluate their views and opinion.

## 7. Discussion

Many techniques exist for stimulating meaningful discussion in pairs, small groups or the whole class. To create an environment of trust and respect, students might develop their own "rules for discussion". Discussions can be structured in a variety of effective ways. Some topics are appropriate to a formal debate, panel or "*Fish Bowl*" format (i.e., a small group discusses while the rest of the class listens and later makes comments and ask questions).Other topics are better suited to a "*Talking Circle*" (i.e., students sit in two circles, one facing outward and the other inward. They discuss with the person sitting opposite; after a period the teacher asks everyone in the inside circle to move one place to the right and discuss the same topic with a new person). Personal or emotional topics are best discussed in pairs or small groups.

To engage the whole class in a topic, the teacher might use techniques like a "*Talk Around*" (i.e., the teacher asks an open-ended question like "What does dignity mean to you?"or "I feel happy when ..." and each student responds in turn).

A lively method of representing discussion graphically is the "*Discussion Web*". Students sit in a discussion circle and speak one at a time. As they do, they pass a ball of yarn along, letting it unwind in the process. Each person keeps hold of the string whenever it passes through her or his hands. Eventually the group is linked by a web of string, clearly showing the pattern of communication that has gone on within it.

## 8. Visual aids

Learning can be enhanced by the use of blackboards, overhead transparencies, posters, displayed objects, flip charts, photographs, slides, videos and films. As a general rule, information produced on transparencies and charts should be brief and concise, and in outline or list form. If more text is required, use hand-outs. However, visual aids can be overused and should never substitute for engaged discussion and direct student participation.

## 9. Research projects

Child rights topics provide many opportunities for independent investigation. This may be formal research using library or Internet facilities or informational research drawing on interviews, opinion surveys, media observations and other techniques of data gathering. Whether individual or group projects, research develops skills for independent thinking and data analysis and deepens understanding of the complexity of human rights issues.

## 10. Role-plays/Simulations

A role-play is like a little drama played out before the class. It is largely improvised and may be done as a story (with a narrator and key characters) or as a situation (where the key characters interact, making up dialogue on the spot – perhaps with the help of the teacher and the rest of the class). Role-plays have particular value for sensitizing students to the feelings and perspectives of other groups and to the importance of certain issues. Role-plays work best when kept short. Allow enough time for discussion afterwards: it is crucial for children to be able to express themselves about feelings, fears or understandings after such activities, to maximize possible benefits and dissipate negative feelings, if any. Teachers may need to discourage students from becoming their role. Participants should be able to step back from what they are doing, to comment perhaps, or to ask questions. Other members of the class should be able to comment and question too, perhaps even joining in the role-play. Variations on role-plays include mock trials, imaginary interviews, simulation games, hearings and tribunals. These usually have more structure, last longer and require more preparation of both teachers and students.

## 11. Problem Solving

The following shows a more systematic approach to problem-solving:

1. Identify a problem and acknowledge it. Stop any physical or verbal activity and ask the children involved to discuss their behaviour together.
2. Get a description of what happened. Ask the children involved and any bystanders about the events that took place. Give everyone a turn to speak without interruption.

   Positive encouragement, such as a touch or a hug where appropriate, can also ease feelings of anger or guilt. However, it is essential to remain neutral at all times.
3. Explore a range of solutions. Ask those directly involved how this problem can be solved. If the children cannot suggest solutions, the teacher can offer some ideas.
4. Reason out the solutions. Point out how more than one fair solution may often exist. Encourage the children to think of the physical and emotional consequences of these solutions and recall past experiences of a similar nature.
5. Choose a course of action. Seek a mutual agreement on one of the solutions presented.
6. Carry out that action.

## 12. Stories

Stories are invaluable. Young children can learn lessons and morals and remember them vividly if they are associated with a much-loved character in a well-told tale. Such stories can be obtained from published literature on children's tales, from parents and grandparents or even by using one's imagination. A classroom library where resources are available may be useful. In selecting books, it is important to obtain attractive volumes that feature both females and males as multicultural, active and non-stereotyped characters. When reading to the class or showing picture books, point out the good things they show or tell.

## Confronting discrimination

In cases of discriminatory behaviour, solutions are not so easy to find. Usually neither the insulted child nor the offending child has a clear understanding of discrimination. The teacher's actions are especially important in this situation. The teacher should first strongly criticize the discriminatory behaviour and make clear that it is definitely unacceptable. The teacher may offer clear support to the child who was the object of the offence without criticism of his or her anger, fear or confusion, and be firm yet supportive with the child who engaged in the discriminatory behaviour. Teachers should help victimized children realize that negative responses to their gender, appearance, disability, language, race or other aspects are due to unacceptable prejudices; they should also examine with children who were involved and who witnessed the situation the issues at stake. Discuss such incidents also with parents, staff and members of the local community.

This method can be used at all school levels as well as in critical situations outside the school environment. It can be applied to all discriminatory behaviour. Where possible, ethnic diversity in the classroom should be acknowledged, understood and even celebrated at every opportunity. It should be remembered that racism and sexism are usually present in children at a very young age, so this method may be remedial. Teachers should also be aware that they too may harbour discriminatory attitudes and strive diligently to recognize and overcome them.Care should also be taken to make the classroom and school accessible and welcoming to children with disabilities.

## Confidence and social respect

In pre-school and lower primary education, teaching for human rights is aimed at fostering feelings of confidence and respect for self and others. These are the basis for the whole culture of human rights. This makes the teacher's "teaching personality" highly important. A supportive approach at all times will make every activity meaningful, even those not specific to human rights teaching.

## Resolving conflicts

Conflicts often arise, and teachers need to develop a consistent strategy to address them. It is imperative that a teacher remain open to discussion of conflict at all times. Emphasize that a solution can be found to any problem. However, children need to think about a problem in order to find a solution.

All activities should involve both boys and girls. If disagreement arises concerning activities, the class may need to make rules to equalize the situation and break down discriminatory behaviour. Such rules become unnecessary with regular use. Equality can also be improved by changing the way the classroom is arranged or how students line up. It is important to avoid grouping children in ways that reinforce obvious differences. Try to facilitate friendships between students as well as awareness that differences are acceptable and natural.

## Evaluation

Information content and levels of understanding of the students can be tested in standard ways. However, assessing attitudes and attitude change is much harder because of the subjective nature of the judgments involved. Open-ended questionnaires given at repeated intervals are the simplest, but the impressions they provide are fleeting at best. It is equally difficult to evaluate whether the human rights climate of the school community has improved. However, if indicators for success are carefully defined and evaluation is done on a regular basis, changes in the school environment can be monitored and responded to. Engaging students in drawing up checklists to assess individual, classroom and school community practices in child rights terms can be an important learning activity events.

☆☆☆☆☆

# 8 CHAPTER

# EDUCATION FOR CHILD RIGHTS–ACTIVITIES

**"Children require guidance and sympathy far more than instruction".**

***—Annie Sullivan***

It is becoming increasing apparent that gone are the days when teaching was synonymous with lecturing or telling. Learning activities today must reflect child development and child learning. For educating about child rights the following activities can be used by the teacher.

## 1. Appreciating similarities and differences

Children are seated in a circle. One child stands in the middle of the circle and makes a statement that describes himself or herself. For example: "Is wearing a belt" or "Has a sister". Everyone who shares that attribute must change places, including the child in the middle. Whoever is left without a seat becomes the person in the middle and names the next attribute. Children will quickly see that they can be similar and different in many ways. An interesting ending would be to choose a more intangible attribute, such as: "People who are kind". The game usually breaks down at this point because it becomes more difficult to identify such attributes at a glance. Teachers may wish to discuss how people usually recognize such behavioral attributes. **(CRC article 2)**

## 2. In the same boat

Teacher names a category (e.g., month of birth, number of siblings, kind of pet, favourite toy or game) and asks children to form a group with others who share that category with them. Older children can respond to more complex categories (e.g., number of languages spoken, career aspiration, hobby, favourite school subject). The game concludes with the question "What did you learn from this activity?" and a discussion of people's unrecognized similarities and differences. **(CRC article 2)**

## 3. Who am I and what am I like?

"Who Am I?" book—Children begin a book about themselves, with a self-portrait on the cover. Personal pictures, prose and poems can be collected in this book. As children learn to write they can put personal details, questions about themselves and answers to questions in it too. If resources are limited, a book can be made for the whole class with a page or two for each child.

**(CRC articles 6, 7, 8, 12, 13, 30)**

## 4. A circle for talking

Children sit in a circle that includes the teacher and any visitors. The teacher makes an open-ended statement and each student answers in turn. Questions might be one or more of the following-

- What I like best about myself is ...
- I would like to be ...
- My favourite game is ...
- I think my name means ...
- I would like to learn about ...
- I feel happy when ...
- I feel sad when ...
- I want to become more ...
- Some day I hope ... .

Listening without interrupting and sharing time equally are very important. Children can "pass" if they do not wish to speak. Each person remains seated until the activity is over. Answers can be included in the "Who Am I?" book(s). **(CRC articles 8, 12, 13, 14, 17, 31)**

## 5. The lifeline

Each child stretches out a piece of yarn that represents his or her own life. Children then hang on their yarn drawings, stories and objects that convey the important things that have happened to them. This can be done in chronological sequence, or in any order that the child may want. It can also be extended into the future. **(CRC articles 6, 8, 12, 13, 14, 27, 30, 31)**

## 6. Me on the wall/ground

Trace the outline of each child on a large piece of paper (best done lying down) or on the ground. Have the student draw/paint in physical details, and then write around personal and physical qualities (e.g., name, height, weight, what the child would most like to learn or do at school or in adulthood). If you have used papers, pin them up around the wall. Allow all students to learn about each other as well as themselves. **(CRC articles 6, 7, 8, 12, 13, 28, 29, 31)**

## 7. Me and my senses

Have children discuss in the circle, or use a role-play to explore the following statements:

- Hearing helps me to ...
- Seeing helps me to ...
- Smelling helps me to ...
- Touching helps me to ...
- Tasting helps me to ... .

Rephrase the questions, where appropriate, to suit the needs of children with disabilities (e.g., "Not being able to see (very well? at all?) I am still me, and I can . . ."). Get each child to invent an instrument to help them hear, smell or touch better. Have them describe, draw or dramatize it. **(CRC articles 23, 26, 28, 29)**

## 8. Wishing-circle

Arrange the students in a circle. Propose that each child in turn makes the following wishes (this can also be done in small groups or pairs):

- If I could be any animal, I would be _______ because ...
- If I could be a bird, I would be _______ because ...
- If I could be an insect, I would be _______ because ...
- If I could be a flower, I would be _______ because ...
- If I could be a tree, I would be _______ because ...
- If I could be a piece of furniture, I would be _______ because ...
- If I could be a musical instrument, I would be _______ because ...
- If I could be a building, I would be _______ because ...
- If I could be a car, I would be _______ because ...
- If I could be a street, I would be _______ because ...
- If I could be a town/province/region, I would be ____ because ...
- If I could be a foreign country, I would be _______ because ...
- If I could be a game, I would be _______ because ...
- If I could be a record, I would be _______ because ...
- If I could be a TV show, I would be _______ because ...
- If I could be a movie, I would be _______ because ...

- If I could be a food, I would be _______ because ...
- If I could be any colour, I would be _______ because ... .

**(CRC articles 13, 14)**

### 9. Imaginary friend

The children sit or lie down quietly with their eyes closed. Tell them to breathe in deeply and then breathe out slowly. Repeat two more times. Now tell them to imagine a special place, a favourite place, anywhere in the world (or even in outer space). Say that they are walking in that place – in their imagination – feeling and hearing and seeing what is going on there. Lead them to a house or building they can visualize, where they go in to find a special room. The room has a door in one wall that opens by sliding up. The door slides up slowly, and as it does so, it reveals a special friend they have never met before – first feet, and finally the face.

This friend can be old or young – anything. This friend is always there, and whenever they need someone to talk to, to turn to, they can visit him or her again if they wish. Close the door, leave the house and come home to the class. Let the children share what they have imagined in a speaking circle or in pairs or groups.**(CRC article 15)**

### 10. Letters and friends

Set up a letter or electronic mail exchange with another class in another school or even another country. Initiate this exchange by sending poems or gifts from the class. This may lead to a visit later if the distance allows, and a chance to meet the children of the other community. Investigate the twin school:

- How big is it?
- What games are played there?
- What do the parents do?
- What are the differences and similarities? **(CRC articles 13, 17, 29)**

### 11. Buddy

Teachers should arrange for their students to have an older buddy from an upper class. An activity should be arranged to encourage children to seek out the help of their buddy if they have a problem. Ways should be devised to encourage the senior buddy to take an interest in his or her small colleague by showing games and helping with activities. **(CRC article 15)**

### 12. People around me

Ask children in a talking circle to think of a good quality in themselves or ask "What are some qualities we admire in people?" Then lead a discussion on these topics:

- Do you respect in others the quality you like about yourself?
- Do you respect good qualities in others that you do not have?
- Do all human beings deserve respect? Why?
- How do you show respect for others?

Next ask children to think of a time when they felt hurt because someone did not respect them.

- How did disrespect feel?
- Why do people sometimes act disrespectfully to others?
- What is dignity? Is your dignity hurt when others do not respect you?
- What can you do when others do not respect you?Finally,
- Ask "What does it mean if we say that all human beings deserve respect?"
- Ask for examples of how life in their community could be more peaceful if people showed greater respect for each other.
- Ask children to think of one way they could show respect for someone.

**(CRC articles 2, 12, 13, 14, 16, 29)**

## 13. The washing machine

Have the children form two parallel lines close together, and facing each other. Send a child from one end between the lines ("through the wash"). Everyone (where this is culturally appropriate) pats him or her on the back or shakes his or her hand while offering words of praise, affection and encouragement. The result is a sparkling, shining, happy individual at the end of the "wash". He or she joins a line, and the process is then repeated for another child. (Running one or two people through daily is more fun than washing everybody in one big clean-up.) **(CRC article 2)**

## 14. Blind trust

Divide the class into pairs. Have one child blindfold the other and have the sighted member of the pair lead the "blind" one about for a few minutes. Make sure the leading child is not abusing the power to lead, since the idea is to nurture trust, not to destroy it. The "leader" of the pair should try to provide as wide a variety of experiences as possible, such as having the "blind" partner feel things with his or her feet or fingers, leading with vocal directions or even playing a game. After a few minutes have the children reverse the roles and repeat the process so that the "leader" is now the led, and the "blind" partner is now the sighted one. Once the activity is over, allow the children to talk about what happened. Discuss how they felt – not just as "blind" partners but their feelings of responsibility as "leaders" too. This can lead not only to a greater awareness of what life is like for people with sight (or hearing) disabilities, but to a discussion of the importance of trust in the whole community. This can lead in turn to a discussion of world society, how it works and how it can fail to work too.

**(CRC articles 3, 23)**

## 15. Creating classroom rules

The importance of classroom climate and the need for participation and cooperation cannot be emphasized enough. The children's suggestions and opinions are also very helpful in creating the best classroom atmosphere. Be open to their help and provide necessary changes. The next activity is very significant because it has a direct effect on classroom climate. It clearly demonstrates a teacher's willingness to involve the class in how the classroom is run and her or his own trust in its members. It also makes children think about what rules are desirable and possible in class, how they might be observed and the teacher's own role in maintaining the classroom environment.

### a. Classroom needs

Classroom rules can be created in a number of ways: as a brainstorm (paring down the results in subsequent discussion);in small groups that then present their findings to a plenary session of the whole class; or as individual assignments that the teacher collates for class consideration later. A good way to begin is by asking children what they "want" (the list may become quite long). Then ask them to choose from this list the items they think are really needed. They should end up with something shorter and much more essential. List these on a chart labelled "Our Classroom Needs". Finally, ask them to choose from their "needs" what they think they have a "right" to expect as members of society. List these on a chart labelled "Our Classroom Rights". Ask why they have chosen as they have. **(CRC articles 12, 13, 28, 29)**

### b. Classroom responsibilities

Emphasize the essential connection between rights and responsibilities. After students have created the list of classroom rights, ask them to rephrase each right in terms of responsibilities and list these in a separate chart labelled "Our Classroom Responsibilities" (e.g., "Everyone should feel safe in this room" might be revised as "Everyone has the responsibility not to insult anybody or hurt anyone's feelings"). **(CRC article 29)**

### c. Living with rights and responsibilities

Once the class has agreed on its lists of basic rights and responsibilities, display them so that they can be referred to or amended as necessary. Sometimes children or the teacher may break the rules or situations may arise that the rules do not address. Sometimes conflicts may arise when classroom rules are not compatible with the rules of other teachers or the school administration. These situations call for discussion and careful consideration of why things are going wrong. Order achieved by general consensus rather than simple control is always harder to get, and the process of reaching this consensus calls for compromise and careful negotiation. Such a process is itself a valuable learning experience. **(CRC articles 12, 13, 28, 29)**

## 16. Understanding child rights

Having arrived at some classroom rules, it is a natural next step to consider the same sort of thing on a universal scale.

### a. Planning for a new country

Explain that a new land has been discovered that has everything needed to sustain human life. No one has ever lived there before. There are no laws and no history. The whole class will be settling there. A small group has been appointed to draw up a list of rights for children for this all-new country. You do not know what position you will have in the new country. Working in small groups, students in each group give this country a name and list ten rights the whole group can agree upon. Each group presents its list and the whole class makes a "class list" that includes all the rights mentioned.Discuss the class list (e.g., what would happen if some rights were excluded? Have any important rights been left out? How is this list different from your classroom rules?) **(UDHR articles 13, 21, 26; CRC articles 12, 13)**

### b. What are children's rights?

Ask students whether there are rights and responsibilities that apply more specifically to them, not just as people but as young people – as children. What might it be wrong to do (or not to do) to someone just because he or she happens, at that point in time, to be "a child"? Introduce the Convention on the Rights of the Child, explaining that it guarantees to children the things they need to grow up healthy, safe and happy and to become good citizens in their community. Help children understand the relationship between needs and rights.

Discuss:

- Why do you think the United Nations has adopted a document just for children's human rights? How are children's needs different from those of adults?
- Why do children need special protection? Give some examples?
- Why do children need special provisions for their welfare.
- What do children need for their survival, happiness and development?
- Why do children need to participate in their communities?
- Give some examples.
- Who is responsible for seeing that children's rights are respected? (e.g., parents? teachers? other adults? Other children? the Government?)

**c. Introducing the Convention on Child Rights**

- Introduce them on Child Rights explaining that it is a list of rights for all children in the world. Then read the simplified version aloud (see annex 1). If students hear an article that matches one of the rights on the class list, write the number of that article next to the right. After completing the reading, discuss the results:

- Were any rights in the Convention on Child Rights left off the class list? Do students now want to add any new rights to the list?
- Were any rights on the class list left out of the Convention on Child Rights?

**(CRC article 29)**

**d. Wants and needs**

Ask children working in small groups to create ten cards that illustrate things that children need to be happy. They can cut pictures from old magazines or draw these things. Help them label the cards. Each group explains and posts its cards under the heading "Needs".

Next announce that the new Government has found that it can only provide some of the items on the list, so the group must eliminate ten items from the list of needs. Remove the cards selected and post them under the heading "Wants".

Then announce that still further cuts are required and the group must eliminate another ten items and follow the same procedure.

**Finally discuss this activity:**

- What items were eliminated first? Why?
- What is the difference between wants and needs?
- Do wants and needs differ for different people?
- What would happen if the class had to go on eliminating needs?

Conclude by explaining that children's rights are based on what all children need to live a healthy, happy life and grow up to be responsible citizens. Introduce the Convention on the Rights of the Child as an effort to make sure that all children have these rights (see activity "What are children's rights?" above). Older children might read aloud the summarized version of the Convention and compare it to their list of wants and needs.

**e. What does a child need?**

Working in small groups, students draw a large outline of a child (or outline one of them) and give the child a name. They then decide on the mental, physical, spiritual and character qualities they want this ideal child to have as an adult (e.g., good health, sense of humour, kindness) and write these qualities inside the outline. They might also make symbols on or around the child to represent these ideal qualities (e.g., books to represent education).

Outside the child, the group lists the human and material resources the child will need to achieve these qualities (e.g., if the child is to be healthy, it will need food and health care). Each group then "introduces" its new member of the community and explains its choices for the child.

Introduce the Convention on the Rights of the Child (see activity "What are children's rights?" above). Then read aloud the summarized version of the Convention. When children hear an article that guarantees a child, each of the needs they have listed, they write the number of the article next to that item. Circle any needs identified by the class but not covered by the Convention.

**f. Promoting children's rights**

In some countries children's rights are advertised by newspapers, radio and television. Ask students working in small groups to make up some advertisements for particular articles of the Convention on the Rights of the Child (e.g., posters, skits, songs or other forms). Ask each group to perform or exhibit their ideas for the class as a whole.

**17. Protecting children**

Look through the Convention on the Rights of the Child and list all the articles that offer protection to children and the circumstances and specific forms of abuse and exploitation that these articles mention.

- Are there others that you might add?
- Are some children more vulnerable and in need of protection than others?

**Discuss responsibility for protecting children:**

- According to the Convention, who has the responsibility for protecting children?
- Does the Convention give any order of priority for this responsibility?
- What happens when those responsible for protecting children fail to do so?
- Research child protection in your community, using the list generated at the beginning of this activity.
- What are children's particular needs for protection in your community?
- What people or groups are providing protection for them?
- Are there ways you and your class can contribute to this less protection?
- Why do you think that the rights of children needed to be expressed in a special human rights treaty?

**(CRC articles 2, 3, 6, 8, 11, 16, 17, 19, 20, 22, 23, 32, 33, 34, 35, 36, 37, 38)**

## 18. Role-play (Summit)

Role-play a summit discussion between the leaders of all countries about a critical issue, for example reduction in the use of land mines or the protection of children from dangerous work. Stage a classroom debate on the topic, with groups working together as the countries involved: some groups trying to ban these practices, some groups refusing to ban. Compare, when feasible, the discussions that led to the Convention on the Prohibition of Anti-Personnel Mines (1997) or the Convention concerning the Prohibition of the Worst Forms of Child Labour (International Labour Organization's Convention No. 182, 1999). Emphasize that different countries and people can work together in ways that allow all of us to live together in peace.

**(CRC articles 3, 4)**

## 19. Packing your suitcase

One of the common results of war and oppression is the creation of refugees, people who flee their home countries because of a "well-founded fear of persecution for reasons of race, religion, nationality, membership in a particular social group or political opinion" (article 1.A.2 of the Convention relating to the Status of Refugees, 1951).

**READ THIS SCENARIO:**

Your partner disappears and is later found murdered. Your name appears in a newspaper article listing suspected subversives. Later you receive a letter threatening your life because of your alleged political activities. You decide you must flee. Pack your bag. You can take only five categories of things (e.g., toiletries, clothing, photographs) and only what you can carry in one bag by yourself. You have five minutes to make these decisions. Remember that you may never return to your home country again.

Ask several students to read their lists. If they omit the newspaper article or the threatening letter (the only concrete proof to offer authorities in the new country that they are fleeing a "well-grounded fear of persecution"), say "Asylum denied". After a few such examples, explain the definition of a refugee and the importance of proof of persecution. Discuss the experience of making emotional decisions in a state of anxiety.

### Research refugees in the world today:

- Where are the greatest concentrations of refugees?
- Where are they fleeing from and why?
- Who is responsible for caring for them?

**(CRC article 22)**

## 20. Child soldiers

In some parts of the world, boys and girls, even younger than ten years old, are recruited to serve as soldiers. Often these children are kidnapped and forced into this dangerous work, which can lead to death, maiming and alienation from their home communities and society as a whole. A new Optional Protocol (2000) to the Convention on the Rights of the Child bans the involvement of children in such armed conflict, as does the International Labour Organization's Convention concerning the Prohibition of the Worst Forms of Child Labour (1999).

**Discuss:**

- Why would armed forces want to use children in warfare?
- What human rights of these children are being violated? Cite particular articles of the Convention on the Rights of the Child.
- How might being a child soldier affect girls and boys differently?
- If a child manages to survive and return to the home community, what are some difficulties that she or he might face at first? In the short term? In the long term?

**Here are some ways in which students can take action or explore the issue further:**

- Find out more about child soldiers in different parts of the world;
- Find out what organizations are working to rehabilitate former child soldiers and offer them support;
- Write letters encouraging the Government to ratify the Optional Protocol to the Convention on the Rights of the Child banning the involvement of children in armed conflict.

**(CRC articles 3, 6, 9, 11, 32, 34, 36, 37, 38, 39)**

## 21. a) Councils and courts

Laws are made by national law-making bodies. Students need to see the process of law-making for themselves in order to answer these questions:

- What is "the law"?
- Who makes it? and Why?

Arrange for a class visit to a regional or central chamber of the country's parliament in session so that students can watch its members at work. Discuss the three questions above. Likewise, arrange a visit to a law court to see not only laws being administered but also decisions being made that set legal precedents which may directly or indirectly affect future decisions. Discuss the same questions above.

If the suggested visits are not possible, or even if they are, organize the class into a model parliament and arrange a debate on current issues or a mock trial to adjudicate a local or national case at law. Encourage students to find suitable examples themselves. To introduce an international dimension, teachers could have the class research the decision making processes of the United Nations and the issues currently discussed. They could also review some cases brought before international commissions, tribunals and courts.

You may also wish to invite a local political figure to talk to the class about the three questions raised at the beginning of this activity, plus three more:

- Why are laws obeyed?
- How is "justice" done? And
- How is "fairness" achieved in government and the law?

Examine article 12 of the Convention on the Rights of the Child, which gives children the right to an opinion in matters that affect them. Has this right been recognized in the courts of your country? How?

**b. Sorts of courts**

Legislative processes can also be learned by arranging the class into an informal court. The "disputants" can be in the middle, with their "friends" and "family" close by and the rest of the class in a circle around them as a "village". Appoint a "magistrate" outside the circle as someone to be turned to only when the locals want an outsider's opinion. Have the disputants put their cases in turn, allowing everybody to elaborate their points. The discussion should continue until a consensus verdict is reached. The issue to be dealt with can be chosen by the teacher with the students' help. Discuss afterwards how the "law" has worked here in both the formal and the informal cases. Note how it may be impossible to find someone to blame, particularly when each party has reasonable points to make. **(CRC articles 3, 12)**

**c. Equality before the law**

Article 7 of the Universal Declaration begins: "All are equal before the law ..." However, this statement of principle is not always reflected in practice.

**Discuss:**

- Are all equal before the law in your community, or are some people treated in different ways?
- What factors might give some people an advantage over others?
- Why is equality before the law essential for a human rights culture? **(CRC article 2)**

**d. Comparing "rights" documents**

Point out that rights are guaranteed not only by international documents like the CRC but also by regional, national and local law codes such as national constitutions. Give students copies of the CRC and any two other documents and ask them to compare whether each contains the following rights and to identify the relevant article(s):

1. Right to education
2. Freedom of expression
3. Equality of all persons
4. Freedom from torture and inhumane treatment
5. Freedom of thought, conscience and religion
6. Adequate food
7. Adequate shelter
8. Adequate health care
9. Right to clean air and water

**Discuss:**

- What similarities and differences did you discover? How can you explain these?
- Does your Constitution or local law include more orf ewer rights than the CRC?
- Did the writers of these documents seem to have the same concept of what "rights" mean?
- Do all documents contain responsibilities as well as rights?
- Do citizens of your country have any rights besides those included in your Constitution or local law?
- What happens when these laws conflict?
- What should be the limits and responsibilities of Governments in guaranteeing their citizens certain rights?
- Should any of the rights listed be guaranteed by all Governments? **(CRC articles: all)**

## 22. Words that wound

Article 13.2.a of the Convention on the Rights of the Child gives a child the right to freedom of expression but specifically restricts expression that violates the rights and reputations of others. Should limits be placed on what we can say about our thoughts and beliefs? Should we always be able to say whatever we like? For the following activity the teacher's discretion is advised.

Give everyone slips of paper and have them write down hurtful comments they hear at school, each on a separate paper. Make a scale on the wall ranging from "Teasing/Playful" to "Extremely Painful/Degrading". Ask students to put their words where they think they belong on the scale (alternatively, papers can be collected and read by the teacher in order to ensure that inputs remain anonymous – students would then put them on the scale). Then ask everyone to examine the wall silently. Usually the same words will appear several times and almost always be rated at different degrees of severity. Discuss this experience: ask students to categorize the words(e.g. appearance, ability, ethnic background, sexuality).

- Are some words only for girls? For boys?
- What conclusions can be drawn about abusive language from these categories?
- Why did some people think a particular word was very painful and others find it playful?

  Divide the class into small groups and give each group several of the words considered most painful. Ask someone in each group to read the first word or phrase. The group should accept that this is a hurtful comment and discuss (1) whether people should be allowed to say such things (2) what to do when it happens. Repeat for each word or phrase. Finally discuss with the class the rights and responsibilities involved in abusive language. Does a teacher have a responsibility to stop hate speech at school?

- Do students have a responsibility to stop it in their own lives? If so, why?
- What can you do in your community to stop hate speech?
- Why is it important to do so? **(CRC articles 12, 13, 14, 16, 17, 29)**

## 22. Growing maturity

The Convention on the Rights of the Child gives children the right to freedom of thought, conscience and religion, according to their growing maturity. Ask students to debate when a young person is sufficiently mature to practice a religion or hold political views that differ from those of the family, culture or tradition. Who should decide? **(CRC article 14)**

## 23. The right to privacy

Article 16 of the Convention on the Rights of the Child gives a child the right to protection from interference with privacy, family, home and correspondence and from libel or slander. However, like many other rights guaranteed to children in the Convention, the extent to which it can be exercised depends on the child's "evolving capacity". Certainly a seven-year-old is not ready to have the same rights and responsibilities as a seventeen-year-old.

### a. When is "old enough"?

**Read the following story to the class:**

Eku and Romit met when they sat side by side at primary school. They soon became best friends, but their friendship had a problem. Their families belonged to different social groups that had a long history of distrust. So when Romit asked if Eku could visit, both parents firmly refused. Eku's family spoke to the teacher and had the friends seated separately. However, their friendship continued until Eku was sent away to finish secondary school in another town. The friends promised to write, but whenever a letter from Eku arrived, Romit's parents destroyed it before Romit could even open it. Romit understands his parents' feelings but also thinks that at sixteen you are old enough to choose your own friends and entitled to have letters kept private.

**Discuss:**

- What rights does Romit have according to the Convention on the Rights of the Child?
- How can Romit's "evolving capacity" be determined?
- What rights do Romit's parents have? Strategize how this conflict might be resolved.
  **(CRC articles 5, 16)**

## 24. Child Rights Club

How does a community maintain itself and flourish? In part, by having its members meet together and organize their affairs. These freedoms make communal involvement very important. Their denial would deprive a society of one of its richest resources: the skills and talents of its own people. Habits of communal participation can be fostered throughout a student's schooling. Opportunities for community service outside the school can also become the basis for a lifelong contribution to social and political affairs. Many schools have student councils that allow participation in their affairs, though the adult hierarchy usually limits what can be done in practice.

A direct experience of working together for something worthwhile may be achieved from having the class form a club to promote human rights. The teacher can initiate a number of relevant tasks aimed at establishing such a club:

- Define the purpose of the Child Rights Club in more detail;
- Hold a competition for a club symbol;
- Make individual membership cards that carry this logo;
- Organize office-holders;
- Put up a special notice board for Child Rights Club activities;
- Find out about national and international Child rights networks and organizations with which the club can liaise; ask for their publications and display these where people can use them;
- Begin holding meetings – the first could discuss the right to freedom of association itself: "Why organize? Why it is important to take part in public affairs, locally, nationally and beyond?"
- Invite guest speakers (e.g., local politicians, issue specialists, area specialists) to give short talks and hold discussions;
- Set up sub-committees to meet and to research particular tasks;
- Commemorate International Child Rights Day, 10th November; find out about other International Days related to human rights and commemorate them. A group could approach other classes with offers to speak to them about particular child rights issues/areas, explaining why the club was formed and what it does, and offering associate membership; where resources permit, the club could also publish a regular newsletter.

**(CRC article 15)**

## 25. Discrimination – stereotypes

In confronting stereotypes, point out the danger of encouraging their opposite. Insist that any grain of truth there may be in a stereotype is just that – a grain. Alternatively, ask the class about occasions on which they may have heard such expressions as "They're all alike, aren't they" or "That lot are all the same".

### a.They are all alike

Give each student a small stone or some other ordinary object, such as a potato, and ask them to become "friends" with it – really get to know it. Ask a few to introduce their "friend" to the class, and to tell a story about how old it is, whether it is sad or happy, or how it got its shape. They can write essays on the subject, songs or poems of praise. Then put all the items back in a box or bag and mix them up together. Tip them out and have the students find their "friend" from among the common lot. Point out the obvious parallel: any group of people seem to be alike at first, but once you get to know them, they are all different, they all have life-histories and they are potentially all friends. This means, however, suspending any stereotypes (like "rocks are cold and hard and indifferent") long enough to get to know them. It means not prejudging them. **(CRC article 2)**

### b. Spot the difference

**Present the following statements:**

1. I like doctors because they are always kind.
2. I like the fact that some doctors are kind to me.
3. Doctors are a kind lot.

Discuss which is the stereotype (No. 3), which is the prejudice (No. 1), and which is merely the statement of opinion (No. 2).Point out how all three statements (as mental frames of reference) will make it harder to appreciate doctors not only as kind and caring people, but as cross and impatient ones too! Discuss how stereotype, prejudice and opinion predetermine attitudes. **(CRC article 2)**

### c. Sex or gender?

Explain the difference between sex (biologically determined factors) and gender (culturally determined factors). Divide students into two teams and ask each to make a list of differences between males and females, some based on sex (e.g., adult men have beards; women live longer) and others based on gender (e.g., men are better at mathematics; women are timid). Each team in turn reads one of its characteristics and the panel must decide whether it is a difference based on sex or gender. Of course, disagreements will arise (e.g., are men naturally more aggressive?) but the resulting discussion will help students to recognize their own gender stereotypes. Examine the classroom, textbooks, media and community for examples of gender stereotyping. **(CRC article 2)**

**d. What I like/What I do**

**Ask students to write out answers to these questions about themselves:**

1. Three things that my sex is supposed to do that I like.
2. Three things that my sex is supposed to do that I don not like.
3. Three things that I would like to do or be if I were of the other sex.

Ask students to share their lists with a partner of the same sex. Then ask each pair to share with a pair of the opposite sex (or in same-sex classrooms, with another pair).

Discuss the results. How does this community respond to people who don't conform to gender expectations? Do gender expectations limit people's human rights?

**(CRC article 2)**

## 26. The Right to Education

Although everyone has the right to education, many never receive an education that fulfills article 29 of the Convention on the Rights of the Child and fosters "the development of the child's personality, talents and mental and physical abilities to their fullest potential" **(CRC, article 29.1).**

**a. Who is not in our school?**

Millions of children never have the opportunity to attend school at all. Many factors exclude them, such as their social status, their sex, or poverty which forces them to work to survive. Lack of education also limits their ability to enjoy other human rights.

Ask students to consider what young people are not represented in their school, for example:

- many girls or boys?
- children with physical disabilities?
- children with mental disabilities?
- children who have been in trouble with the law or the school authorities?
- children who are orphaned?
- homeless children?
- children of migrant workers?
- refugee children?
- children of minority groups in the community?
- poor children whose families need them to work?

**For each group mentioned as absent from their school, ask:**

- Why don't these children attend this school? Should they? Why or why not?
- Do they attend school elsewhere?
- What about children who cannot physically attend a school? How do they get an education?

**If some children named attend different schools, ask:**

- Why do these children attend a different school from yours?
- Where is this school? Can children get there easily?
- Must families pay for their children to attend this school? What if the parents cannot afford this alternative school?
- Do you think children get a good education there?

Ask how the right to education can be made available to those children who do not attend school (e.g., poor children whose families need them to work; girls who marry or have children while still of school age). Whose responsibility is it to ensure that they receive an education?

If possible, have students research and perhaps visit some schools for students with special needs. Have students discuss or write about whether these alternative schools meet the standards of the Convention of the Rights of the Child regarding the child's right to education. What can they do to advocate for the rights of all children to an education?

**(CRC articles 28, 29)**

**b. What if you could not read?**

Ask students to make a list of all the times they read something in a normal day: at home, at school, in the community or anywhere. They should include such "unconscious reading" as that done while using a computer, watching television and walking in the neighbourhood.

Ask students to compare their lists and discuss:

- How would your life be affected if you could not read?
- What activities would you be unable to do or do well?
- How could illiteracy affect the health, safety and security of you and your family?
- How would you be affected if you could not read and you were a Mother? / Father?
  - Factory worker?
  - Agricultural worker?
  - Shop owner?
  - Soldier?
  - Citizen?

The right to education illustrates the principle of the interdependency of human rights. Ask the class to consider the summarized version of the Convention of the Rights of the Child and ask "How would your ability to enjoy this right be different if you had no education?"

Point out that, among the approximately 113 million children in the world who are not benefiting from primary education, 60 per cent are girls. Ask students to explain these statistics. How does this fact affect the human rights of women and girls?
**(CRC article 13)**

### 27. An adequate standard of living

Adequate food and water are basic development priorities. Article 27 of the Convention on the Rights of the Child guarantees every child the right to a standard of living adequate for her or his physical, mental, spiritual, moral and social development. These rights in turn are a concern of such bodies as the United Nations Children's Fund (UNICEF) and the Food and Agriculture Organization of the United Nations (FAO) and have a bearing also on national security and world peace. Ask students to research the minimum requirements for food and water necessary for survival and for well-being.What happens when a child lacks a standard of living adequate for full development?

Assign students countries with contrasting levels of development to research using United Nations statistics from publications such as UNICEF's *State of the World's Children* or the United Nations Development Programme's *Human Development Report.* Have each student present a profile of an average person from that country (e.g. life expectancy, income, diet, and access to clean water). Discuss the effects of such differences on the development of individuals as well as nations and regions. Teachers of materially privileged students might ask them to find out about poverty in their own communities. Discuss who bears responsibility for protecting people from the effects of poverty. **(CRC articles 6, 27)**

### 28. Effects webs

Young people today need to understand the world as a complex web of interdependent relationships and appreciate the delicate balance among the parts of that web, so that changing any one part affects the whole. For example, environmental pollution in one place can affect food chains, health, living conditions and livelihoods in many other places. Issues too are interrelated. Poverty may be caused by many factors, and any efforts to eradicate poverty must consider all of them. To help students appreciate the complexity of these interrelationships, divide the class into an even number of small groups and assign each a statement, with at least two groups receiving the same statement. These sentences should express either a fact (e.g., "In ___ at least 30 per cent of the population is infected with the HIV-AIDS virus") or a "what if" statement (e.g., "What if women owned as much property as men?"). Each group writes its statement at the top of a piece of chart paper. Below the statement, they should write three consequences of that statement (e.g., "The parents of many children will die", "Many children will be born infected with HIV-AIDS", "National health care services will be overburdened by so many sick people"). Then below each of these three statements, write three consequences resulting from each (e.g., "The parents of many children will die" might lead to "Families and social services will be overburdened caring for orphaned children", "There will be fewer workers available", "There will be many children without parents to raise them properly"). The result is a graphic web of effects that could be developed even further. Ask groups with the same statement to compare and discuss their work. Display the charts and make a "gallery walk" so students can explain their webs to other members of the class. Discuss the human rights and child rights implications of these webs and how single issues affect many aspects of society and many different countries. **(CRC article 3)**

### 29. A model United Nations simulation

Select a few current issues of global importance for students to focus on. Assign individuals or groups of students to represent and research a variety of United Nations Member States. Explain that the goals of their research are to understand the assigned country and how it would regard the key issues. When students have had time to complete their research, ask each "ambassador" to write a resolution for the "General Assembly" on one of the key issues of importance in their country or region. The resolution should include a detailed description of the problem and a plan to improve the situation, including what role the United Nations should play. Students will need to convince others that their resolution benefits everyone and deserves to be considered.

Encourage students to compare their resolutions and begin to seek supporters and/or co-sponsors. Explain that they need to be prepared to amend their resolutions and build consensus to get them passed. Hold a mock United Nations forum. Seat students in a circle with the names of their countries in front of them. The teacher or a capable student serves as "Secretary-General". Establish some rules of order for the forum (e.g., each person is addressed as "The Ambassador from ___" ; no one may speak unless recognized by the "Secretary-General"). The "Secretary-General" calls for resolutions to be presented, debated, questioned and voted upon. After discussion on a potential resolution, anyone may move that the resolution be put to the vote. For a motion to pass, it must be seconded by any other "ambassador". A two-thirds majority is needed to pass a resolution. Conclude the simulation with a written or oral evaluation, including both a self-evaluation and an assessment of what students learned about the United Nations and its role in world affairs. **(CRC article 3)**

☆☆☆☆☆

# 9 CHAPTER

# CHILD RIGHTS BASED APPROACH

**"We worry what a child will become tomorrow, yet we forget he/she is someone today".**

—*Stacia Staucher*

Everyone has human rights, including adults and children. Children's rights are simply specific human rights for all children and young people from birth to 18 years of age. They are needed because they reflect the special status of childhood - a period of rapid change and development during which this group experiences different vulnerabilities (e.g. physical weakness or lack of knowledge) and therefore has different entitlements from adults.

Our explanation of what childhood is and recognition of this special status has been developed over a long period time. Right through history, children have been abused and exploited. They suffer from hunger and homelessness; work in harmful conditions, high infant mortality, deficient health care and limited opportunities for basic education. A child need not live such a life. Childhood can and **must** be preserved. Children have the right to survive, develop, be protected and participate in decisions that impact their lives. Aries (1962), and other theorists who have come after him, tells us that the idea of childhood is **socially constructed**. This means that people tend to see children either as potential victims who need looking after, or as potential threats who need to be controlled. One of the consequences of our current thinking is that children and young people are seen as passive and helpless and adults must 'do something' to help. This has been translated into the understanding that children and young people in need of care should be 'taken away', 'be properly educated' or 'get the right kind of treatment.' This thinking focuses on children and young people's weaknesses and not their strengths.

## THE UN CONVENTION: ADDRESSING CHILDREN'S RIGHTS GLOBALLY

World interest in the rights of children coalesced in 1989, when the UN Convention on the Rights of the Child was drafted. The UN Convention on the Rights of the Child [UNCRC] is the most comprehensive human rights document ever adopted by the international community. Forty-two countries spent 10 years drafting the *Convention*. All but two countries in the world — the United States and Somalia — have ratified it. Built on varied legal systems and cultural traditions, the *Convention* is a universally agreed set of non-negotiable standards and obligations linking the child and fundamental human rights. Notably, the *Convention* is the first legally binding international instrument to incorporate the full range of human rights — civil, political, economic, social and cultural, and it is the most comprehensive treaty for the protection and support of children in existence today. The *Convention* is also the only international human rights treaty that gives NGOs an explicit role in monitoring its implementation.

The *Convention* legally guarantees all children:

- The right to survival.
- The right to develop to the fullest.
- The right to protection from harmful influences, abuse and exploitation.
- The right to participate fully in family, cultural and social life

The UNCRC emphasizes strengths and asks adults to see children and young people as active and not passive objects. Through the UNCRC, children are **rights-holders**.

## ADOPTING A RIGHTS-BASED APPROACH: WHAT DOES THIS MEAN?

There are five major consequences of employing a rights-based approach to children's survival, growth, development, protection and participation:

**Rights are not charity.** Children do not seek rights as petitioners of the goodwill of society. Rather, governments, the voluntary sector, community institutions, and parents and caregivers, are accountable for respecting and furthering these rights.

Another way to describe this concept is in terms of "entitlements versus privilege." Among other things, this means that basic services for children must be protected at all times, including during periods of economic reforms and deficit reduction.

**Rights are universal.** The rights guaranteed in the *Convention* are universally applicable; therefore all children have the same rights to survival, growth, development, protection and participation.

**Children's rights are not less important than adult rights.** An important extension of the human rights movement is that children are not the property of parents nor are they less important citizens. The designation of children as bearers of rights is an important step forward in the human rights movement. In addition, because of their particular vulnerability (e.g. children cannot support themselves financially), children's rights should supercede the rights of adults in cases where they may conflict.

**Rights can only be fully realized with empowerment.** In the past, children were viewed as passive beneficiaries of assistance and objects of charity, rather than as active participants in their own development. Now, children are seen as 'protagonists' and 'agents of social transformation.' This change in attitude also initiates a process whereby children, within the context of their evolving capacities, participate in the processes and decisions that concern them and affect their lives.

**Rights are indivisible and interdependent.** One of the basic principles of international human rights law is the indivisibility and interdependence of rights. In other words, the implementation of each right set forth in the *Convention* should take into account the implementation of and respect for, many other rights of the child. The indivisibility and interdependence of rights mirrors what is now known about how children develop, and that the determinants of child development cannot be separated, one from the other, and that action in one area (e.g. health) will affect other areas of development (e.g., learning).

In **RIGHTS-BASED APPROACH decisions** are to be taken after considering the following parameters—

**1. Participation**

Were the views of the child sought? What are they and how can we take them into account? Does the child know how we have considered their views? Have we explored how the child can engage fully in decisionmaking, taking account of their age? Have we offered sufficient support to help them engage? Have we allowed time for preparation and created an environment in which the child is comfortable to speak out? Is the language used appropriate to their developmental level?

**2. Non-discrimination**

Have all options been explored? Are we advocating for this child as a rights holder and is he/she an equal partner in the discussion? Are all relevant persons included in the discussion? Are we making every effort to overcome difficulties, and/or prejudices, including our own, regarding the child or young person being an equal partner?

**3. Best Interests**

Are decisions based on the child or young person's background, future and best interests? Are we being guided by other considerations such as resource issues or organizational constraints? Are we making assumptions about the child based on issues such as our own experience, values and judgments? Are we regularly reviewing the decisions made, and have we taken the opinion of the child or young person into account?

**4. Life, survival and development**

Is the initial decision still safeguarding the survival and development of the child to the maximum extent possible? Is it subject to regular review?

Adults also sometimes comment that 'children and young people know too much about their rights already.' The truth is, however, as Marshall acknowledges, that children and young people know very little about their rights. What they believe they know is often only a fragment or even a caricature, a needs-based approach does not identify anyone who has a clear responsibility to meet needs. In other words, needs – unlike rights – do not create any valid claims on anyone to fulfill them, therefore the fulfillment of needs, instead of being a duty, becomes a charitable action dependent on the goodwill of powerful adults who cannot be held to account if they do not fulfill their duty as this duty is not recognized. By contrast, a rights-based approach focuses on the responsibility and duty of adults under the UNCRC to uphold the minimum requirements of care outlined in the Convention and the relevant

## Applying a Rights-Based Approach to Programming

Applying a rights-based approach to programming means:

- Putting children at the centre, recognising them as **right holders** and social actors,
- Recognising governments as primary **duty bearers** accountable to their citizens – including children – and to the international community,
- Recognising parents and families as **primary care-givers**, protectors and guides and supporting them in these roles,
- Giving priority to children and to a **child friendly environment,**
- Being **gender sensitive** and seeking inclusive solutions which involve a focus on **those** boys and girls who are at risk and who are discriminated against,
- Addressing **unequal power structures** (class, sex, ethnicity, age, caste, religion etc)
- Holding a **holistic vision** of the rights of the child whilst making strategic choices and taking specific actions,
- Setting **goals** in terms of **fulfilment of rights**
- Aiming for sustainable results for children by **focusing** not only on the immediate, but also on the **root causes of problems,**
- Using **participatory and empowering approaches**, in particular regarding children
- Building **partnerships and alliances** for promotion of rights of the child,
- Counting on **international co-operation,**
- Focusing on those who are most at risk and discriminated against,
- Taking a holistic perspective which requires a **multi-sectoral response**
- Providing a long term goal which is clearly set out in **international legal frameworks** that are shared by governments, donors and civil society, and
- Encouraging **legal and other reforms**, such as regular monitoring mechanisms, which create a much greater likelihood of sustainable change.

" Child Rights Programming (CRP) means using the principles of child rights to plan, manage, implement and monitor programmes with the overall goal of strengthening the rights of the child as defined in international law."

## CRP Principles:

The following principles underpin all work on CRP:

- The principle of indivisibility of rights
- The principle of universality of rights
- The four general principles of the Convention of the Rights of the Child:
- The right not to be discriminated against
- The best interests of the child
- The right to survival and development
- The right to be heard
- The principle of children as holders of rights
- The principle of duty bearers

Reflection on CRP principles help ensure a quality focus on meaningful children's participation, for Example:

### • Children as right holders (and the right to be heard):

Are we working with children and young people in ways that respect them as right holders and social actors? Are we providing meaningful opportunities for girls and boys to express their views and for their views to be heard in decisionmaking processes which affect them?

### • Duty Bearers and Accountability:

Are we preparing adult duty bearers (parents, teachers, local and national government officials) to listen to children and young people and be held accountable to them? Are we supporting duty bearers, enhancing their capacity and strengthening their structures and systems so they can effectively respond to children in fulfilling their rights? Children's participation helps guide the interpretation of various CRC articles (e.g., best interests, non-discrimination) and is relevant for all aspects of implementation of the CRC. Participation enables children and young people to increase fulfillment of their rights to survival, protection and development. Their participation transforms the power relations with adults and ends their 'silent status', which has for so long led to the marginalisation, exploitation and abuse of girls and boys. All CRP programming efforts seek to increase opportunities for informing and involving children and young people in all stages of the programme cycle. They also promote realisation of children's participation rights in different settings: family, school, local community, local governance, etc. Furthermore, reflection on CRP Principles helps ensure meaningful participation.

- **Non-discrimination and Universality :**

Are both girls and boys, children with disabilities, children from different religions, castes, tribal groups, street children and so on given equal opportunity to participate? Are we reaching the most marginalised? Are children encouraged to reflect on values of inclusion in their own participation initiatives?

- **Best interests of the child:**

Are we taking children's evolving capacities into consideration, enabling younger children and children with different kinds of abilities to participate to the best of their ability? Are children given enough information to make informed choices about when and to what extent they want to participate? Are parents (and other relevant adults) involved so that they do not feel threatened by children's participation but rather support children's views and actions?

- **Survival and development:**

Are children given clear information so they will not take risks? Do adults create a supportive environment so their participation is conducive to their development? Are we building upon early child development initiatives?

- **Indivisibility:**

Are we working with children and young people in a holistic, cross-sectoral way that enables us to be responsive to whichever right violations they raise?

An ingrained social bias against children's inclusion has traditionally worked against young people's participation throughout South and Central Asia. Gradually we are seeing indications that this situation is beginning to change through initiatives that have been taken at the community level on child focused programmes and policies, as well as at the national level, where advocacy has been utilized to ensure the implementation of child-friendly laws. True citizenship requires children's active and pro-active participation - political participation is the chief element of inclusion and the key to allowing young people to influence the communities around them and to become real stakeholders. This kind of participation gives children access to the issues that concern them most, that is, child rights issues. Children Citizenship

## PRACTICE EXAMPLES USING THE NEEDS VERSUS RIGHTS FRAMEWORK

Two illustrations using the Needs versus Rights framework follow, using examples from the report entitled 'Lets Face It!' which was produced by Who Cares? Scotland.

- **Bullying:**

One of the issues raised by the children and young people in this report was bullying. When dealing with bullying behavior, the focus is often on assisting victims of bullying with their immediate needs. This falls under the needs-led approach. Working with the underlying causes for bullying behavior, possibly by starting life skills training or creative drama sessions with children and young people, could help to address the issue in the longer term, and illustrates a rights-based approach.

● **Restraint**

Misuse of restraint and sanctioning also concerned children and young people in the report. The UNCRC acknowledges the need for discipline but insists it must be administered in a way that is consistent with the child's dignity. It also acknowledges the need for some children and young people to be restrained, but insists that this must conform to the law and be a last resort. Helping children and young people to understand the consequences of behavior and create an environment of reflection and learning is a longer-term solution and can give them valuable skills for the future.

## INDIA'S COMMITMENT TOWARDS CHILDREN'S RIGHTS

India, the post-independence era has experienced an unequivocal expression of the commitment of the government to the cause of children through constitutional provisions, policies, programmes and legislation. The Constitution of India in Article 39 of the Directive Principles of State Policy pledges that "the State shall, in particular, direct its policy towards securing .... that the health and strength of workers, men and women, and the tender age of children are not abused, and that citizens are not forced by economic necessity to enter avocations unsuited to their age or strength, that children are given opportunities and facilities to develop in a healthy manner, and in conditions of freedom and dignity, and that childhood and youth are protected against exploitation, and against moral and material abandonment."

Being a party to the UN declaration on the Rights of the Child 1959, India adopted the National Policy on Children in 1974. Children's programmes have occupied a prominent place in the national plans for human resource development. The Constitution of India, the National Policy for Children, many other policies and legislation accord priority to children's needs. The Government of India ratified the Convention on the Rights of the Child on 2nd December, 1992. sIndia is also a signatory to the World Declaration on the Survival, Protection and Development of Children. In pursuance of the commitment made at the World Summit, the Department of Women and Child Development under the Ministry of Human Resource Development has formulated a National Plan of Action for Children. Most of the recommendations of the World Summit Action Plan are reflected in India's Development under the Ministry of Human Resource Development has formulated a National Plan of Action for Children. Most of the recommendations of the World Summit Action Plan are reflected in India's National Plan of Action.

The National Plan of Action has been formulated keeping in mind the needs, rights and aspirations of 300 million children in the country and sets out quantifiable time limits for India's Charter of Action for Children by 2000 AD. The priority areas in the Plan are health, nutrition, education, water, sanitation and environment. The Plan gives special consideration to children in difficult circumstances and aims at providing a framework, for actualisation of the objectives of the Convention in the Indian context. The National Plan of Action also lists out activities to achieve these goals. To make the aims and activities of the plan more need-based and area-specific, the Central Government has urged the State governments to prepare a Plan of Action for Children for their States, taking into account the regional disparities that may exist. A 'historic' bill making education free and compulsory for all children in the age group of 6 to 14 years has also got Parliament's nod in August, 2009.

☆☆☆☆☆

# 10 CHAPTER

# CHILD SURVIVAL

**"Life affords no greater responsibility, no greater privilege, than the raising of the next generation."** ***—C. Everett Koop***

## INTRODUCTION

India's burgeoning economy has not been kind to the majority of it's children. The disparities between rich and poor are acutely observed in the shocking hunger and malnutrition rates for large numbers of India's children. Even after decades of efforts and government's good intentions, child malnutrition rates in several parts of India are worse than in many sub-Saharan African countries, and they stand out as a paradox in the country.

Of India's one billion plus population 158 million are between 0-6 years. The infant mortality rate in India is 57/1000 live births. The neonatal mortality rate is 39/1000 live births. The stark reality is that almost one in every three babies in the world who die before they are four weeks old is from India. India is home to 40 percent of the world's malnourished children and 35 percent of the developing world's low-birth weight infants; every year, 2 million children die in India, accounting for one in five child deaths in the world. More than half of these deaths could be prevented if children were well nourished. According to the Global Hunger Index (GHI) developed by International Food Policy Research Insitute (IFPRI), which captures three dimensions of hunger- *viz*: insufficient food availability, child malnutrition, and child mortality–India ranks 96th, far behind Brazil (28), China (47), Thailand (58), Vietnam (75), and barely ahead of Bangladesh (102). Nearly two-thirds of India's alarmingly high GHI score is attributable to India's high child malnutrition rate. It is shocking that in child malnutrition India ranks 117th of the 119 countries ranked, right before Bangladesh and Nepal and after countries such as Sudan, Cambodia, and Ethiopia (IFPRI 2008).

Over half of all women in India are anaemic as are 70% of children under the age of five. 22% of all children whose birth weight record is available are low birth weight babies which are a significant contributing factor to malnutrition later in life. The issue of underweight children is particularly serious in rural areas and among poorer families, ethnic minorities, lower castes and other socially marginalized groups. India's public expenditure on health remains abysmally low and in some places financing for child nutrition programs remains unspent. In effect, well-meaning programs have fundamentally failed to deliver.

For over three decades now it has been argued that five inter-connected factors determine the nutritional status of children: Health and nutritional status of the mother during pregnancy, infant care and feeding, prevention of communicable diseases, timely and rational management of childhood illnesses, and persistent poverty, seasonal food shortages and hunger and workload of the mother.

Poverty denies children their rights. It weakens a child's protective environment, as much abuse and exploitation of children is linked to widespread and deeply entrenched poverty. It blights their lives with ill health, malnutrition, and impaired physical and mental development. It saps their energy and undermines their confidence in the future. No society has ever seen a broad-based reduction in poverty without major and sustained investments in the rights of its people to health, nutrition and basic education.

Poverty is transmitted from one generation to the next. Impoverished, malnourished mothers, for example, often give birth to under-weight babies. These babies are more likely to die and, if they do survive, they are less likely to grow and develop to their full potential. Chronic malnutrition, micronutrient deficiencies and frequent illness can lead to poor school performance. Consequently, affected children are more likely to drop out of school early and work at occupations below the poverty line, if they manage to find work at all.

The high proportion of child under-nutrition, combined with the large population base, has made India the country with the largest number of stunted, wasted and underweight children in the world. According to a recent United Nations Children's Fund (UNICEF) estimate, India accounts for 31 per cent of the developing world's children who are stunted and 42 per cent of those who are underweight.

## UNDER-NUTRITION CAUSE FOR CONCERN

There are several reasons why India should do something about child under-nutrition. Most significantly, being well-nourished is the right of every child, and the state has the obligation to ensure proper nutrition for all children. Scientific evidence offers other justifications as well. Undernourished children have significantly lower chances of survival than children who are well-nourished. They are much more prone to serious infections and die from common childhood illnesses such as diarrhoea, measles, malaria, pneumonia, and HIV and AIDS. The risk of dying increases with the severity of the under-nutrition. For instance, a child suffering from severe acute malnutrition is nine times more likely to die than children who are not undernourished.

## 1. The effect of under-nutrition on morbidity, mortality, cognitive and motor development

Through precipitating disease and speeding its progression, malnutrition is a leading contributor to infant, child and maternal mortality and morbidity. It has been estimated to play a role in about half of all child deaths and more than half of child deaths from major diseases, such as malaria, diarrhoea, pneumonia and measles. Nevertheless, it is generally accepted that children who are underweight or stunted are at greater risk for childhood morbidity and mortality, poor physical and mental development, inferior school performance and reduced adult size and capacity for work. Protein-energy malnutrition weakens immune response and aggravates the effects of infection and, so, children who are malnourished tend to have more severe diarrhoeal episodes and are at a higher risk of pneumonia. In addition, malnutrition in early infancy is associated with increased susceptibility to chronic disease in adulthood, including coronary heart disease, diabetes and high blood pressure. Protein-energy malnutrition in early childhood is also associated with poor cognitive and motor development. Iron and Vitamin A deficiencies are leading risk factors for disease in developing countries, especially those with high mortality rates. Iodine deficiency, too, is a mortality risk. Vitamin A Deficiency (VAD) is a well-known cause of morbidity and mortality, especially among young children and pregnant women. In young children, it can cause xerophthalmia and keratomalacia and lead to blindness; limit growth; weaken the immune system, exacerbate infection and increase the risk of death.

## 2. The effect of under-nutrition on schooling, adult productivity and economic growth

The cognitive and physical consequences of under-nutrition – both underweight and micronutrient deficiencies – undermine educational attainment and labor productivity, with adverse implications for income and economic growth.

### Schooling

Malnutrition at any stage of childhood affects schooling and, thus, the lifetime-earning potential of the child. Some of the pathways through which malnutrition affects educational outcomes include a reduced capacity to learn and fewer total years of schooling. Nutrition is important to ensure proper brain formation and development, which starts in the womb, development of the brain goes on during early childhood. Evidence suggests that children who are stunted often enroll late in school, complete fewer grades and perform less well in school. This, in turn, affects their creativity and productivity in later life.

### Adult productivity and economic growth

A few attempts have been made to estimate the productivity losses associated with malnutrition in India. As with the global estimates above, these are intrinsically imprecise, requiring many assumptions and approximations. One study estimates that the productivity losses due to PEM (Protein Energy Malnutrtion), IDD (Iodine Deficiency Disorder), and IDA (Iron Deficiency Anemia), in the absence of appropriate interventions, amounts to around US$114 billion between 2003 and 2012. A more recent study, examining only the productivity losses associated with foregone wage-employment resulting from child malnutrition, estimates the loss to be US$2.3 billion (or Rs.103 billion). Other studies suggest that micronutrient deficiencies alone may cost India US$2.5 billion annually and that the productivity losses (manual work only) from stunting, iodine deficiency and iron deficiency together are responsible for a total productivity loss of almost 3% of GDP. Iodine deficiency is known to affect a child's Intelligence Quotient (IQ) adversely. It has also been established that children with deficient growth before age two are at an increased risk of chronic disease as adults, especially if they gain weight rapidly in the later stages of childhood. A low birth weight baby, who is stunted and underweight in its infancy and gains weight rapidly in childhood and adult life, is much more prone to chronic conditions such as cardiovascular disease and diabetes.

Equally unjust are the levels of inequality that characterize the nutrition situation. Levels of child under-nutrition vary widely across the country. In general, in India, undernourishment is higher among rural than urban children. For instance, in 2005-06, the proportion of underweight children in urban areas was 36 per cent as against 49 per cent in rural areas. Similarly, levels of stunting and wasting are higher in rural than in urban areas.

Levels of child under-nutrition vary widely across Indian States. Less than 22 per cent of the children below five years are underweight in Sikkim and Manipur whereas the proportion is 57 per cent in Jharkhand and 60 per cent in Madhya Pradesh. Similarly, the proportion of underweight children is highest – 55 per cent – among those belonging to the Scheduled Tribes, 48 per cent among those belonging to the Scheduled Castes, 43 per cent among Other Backward Class children and 34 per cent among others. Again, though the levels of under-nutrition are not that dissimilar between boys (42 per cent underweight) and girls (43 per cent), it is well established that girls are discriminated against when it comes to access to food, nutrition, health and care.

## EXPLAINING UNDER-NUTRITION

Several underlying causes explain the prevalence of child under-nutrition. Household income levels and poverty make a difference. In general, we find that levels of child under-nutrition are the lowest in the highest wealth quintile and the highest in the lowest wealth quintile.

Here it is important to view differentials in wealth as an outcome of the inequalities in the distribution of various opportunities – economic, social, political and cultural. As a matter of fact, it is the poverty of opportunities that explains under-nutrition much more effectively than the poverty of incomes *per se*. For instance, levels of child nutrition are better in societies where women enjoy relatively greater opportunities and freedoms and there is greater gender equality. Nutritional outcomes among children are much better where girls have more opportunities to pursue education. Datas show that malnutrition among Indian children below three years born to illiterate mothers (52 per cent) is almost three times higher than levels reported among mothers who have completed 12 years of education (18 per cent).

The pathways of influence between women's education and nutritional well-being could be many. More educated women tend to be better informed, they enjoy better opportunities for employment, they tend to be less superstitious, and they seek out modern health care and advice much more readily than less-educated women. Educated women also tend to have a greater say in decision making within the household, they enjoy greater self-esteem, and they are treated more equally within the household and by society. Along with basic education, the socialising processes of schooling expose girls to several aspects of human life, including the opportunity to make friends, interact, broaden perspectives, consult, and discuss many matters. In the event of an illness or any problem, women who have been to school are in a more advantageous position to find out what is in the best interest of children through a broader process of dialogue and consultations than women who have been denied the freedom to even go to school.

## WHAT NEEDS TO BE DONE

The most significant direct intervention designed by India to tackle under-nutrition is the Integrated Child Development Services (ICDS) programme. Most reviews and assessments have established that the more than 30-year-old programme has not succeeded in delivering the desired result of preventing and eliminating under-nutrition. This is what prompted the Prime Minister in his Independence Day address in 2008 to remark: "The problem of malnutrition is a curse that we must remove."

What then are the actions needed to ensure the eradication of child under-nutrition?

These suggestions fall broadly into three clusters: technical, programmatic requirements, and institutional arrangements.

### 1. Technical interventions

Listed below are such five critical technical interventions.

1. Improve breastfeeding practices in the first six months of life by ensuring that:
   - All newborns start breastfeeding within one hour after birth (early initiation);
   - All newborns are fed the nutrient-rich colostrum in the first three-to-four days of life (colostrum feeding); and
   - All infants are fed only breast milk in the first six months of life (exclusive breastfeeding) and are not fed any other solid or liquid, not even water.
2. Improve foods and feeding practices for children 6-23 months old by ensuring that:
   - Infants are fed complementary foods beginning at about six months of age while breastfeeding continues until two years and beyond;
   - Complementary foods are rich in energy, protein, and micronutrients (vitamins and minerals).
3. Control micronutrient deficiencies and anaemia in the first years of life by ensuring that:
   - All children 6-59 months old are provided with Vitamin A supplements twice a year (about six months apart);

- All children 12-59 months old are provided with deworming tablets twice a year (about six months apart); and

4. Control micronutrient deficiencies and anaemia in adolescent girls and women by ensuring that:
   - Anaemia is prevented in adolescent girls and pregnant women through supplementation programmes with iron and folic acid and deworming tablets;
   - Iodine deficiency is prevented in adolescent girls and women by ensuring that all salt for direct human consumption contains adequate levels of iodine.
5. Provide quality care for children with severe under-nutrition by ensuring that:
   - Cases of severe acute under-nutrition are managed at home with simplified protocols and also clinically (wherever required) under appropriate medical supervision.

**2. Programmatic requirements**

Reviewing the global experience with reducing child under-nutrition, UNICEF has identified seven programme success factors.

1. *Situation analysis*: To understand and analyse the local nutrition situation and its determinants.
2. *Linkages with other sectors*: The package of nutrition interventions need to be implemented in conjunction with relevant health, water and sanitation interventions. Better household food security through strengthened agricultural and social protection programmes is equally essential.
3. *Political commitment and partnership*: Strong and clear government ownership, leadership, commitment, coordination and clarity of roles and responsibilities of several departments.
4. *Capacity-building*: Promotion of early initiation of breastfeeding and exclusive breastfeeding; home visits by community health workers; immunisation and weighing sessions; sick child consultations; and services to prevent mother-to-child transmission of HIV; paediatric AIDS treatment. Review, identify opportunities, update knowledge and strengthen the capacity of health workers in order to extend the effective reach and coverage of the health system.
5. *Communication and community*: Initiate effective large-scale communication strategies and community involvement; offer regular support and counselling of caregivers at the community level; place strong emphasis on quality implementation, monitoring and evaluation.
6. *Corporate social responsibility*: Engage with the private sector, especially with the marketing of appropriately nutritious foods and compliance with the International Code of Marketing of Breastmilk Substitutes and other relevant standards.
7. *Resources*: Ensure that adequate resources – financial and human – are mobilised, allocated and expended on the delivery of nutrition programmes for children.

**3. Institutional arrangements**

Several reports and committees have called for more specific suggestions, including an improved system of monitoring through the use of better indicators, implementation of the ICDS in a mission mode, recognising counselling for infant and young child feeding as a "service" in the ICDS, scaling down focus on food supplementation, supporting innovative child care service delivery options, piloting and universalising a two-anganwadi-worker model in the ICDS, and ensuring better coordination between health and nutrition interventions. Others have called for transferring the responsibility for nutrition from the Ministry of Women and Child Development to the Ministry of Health and Family Welfare. The Coalition for Sustainable Nutrition Security in India has proposed a five-point charter for overcoming the curse of malnutrition.

**1. Institutional structures for public policy and coordinated action in nutrition.**

Recognising the need for concurrent attention to food (macro and micronutrients, clean drinking water) and non-food factors (for example, sanitation, environmental hygiene, primary health care, literacy and income security), set up the following

- Consultative, policy, oversight and monitoring structures.
- A Council for Freedom from Hunger, selected by gram sabhas and local bodies at the panchayat, nagarpalika and local body levels.
- A State-Level Committee on Nutrition Security, chaired by the Chief Minister, with all Ministers concerned and representatives of civil society organisations, the corporate sector and the mass media in every State and Union Territory.
- A Cabinet Committee for Nutrition Security, chaired by the Prime Minister at the national level.

**2. Learning for success: converting the unique into the universal.**

On the basis of evidence and successful programming within India and elsewhere, it will be prudent to place special focus on:

- Child nutrition in the first two years of life; and
- Women's nutrition throughout the life cycle.

**3. Action at local level: community food and nutrition security system.**

❖ Banks by the proposed panchayat and local Council for Freedom from Hunger support.

  - Adopting, wherever hidden hunger from the deficiency of iron, folic acid, iodine, zinc and vitamin A in the diet is endemic, food-cum-micronutrient supplementation and appropriate and effective fortification approaches (as for example, iodine- and iron-fortified salt).

**4. Action at State level: Coordinating nutrition security initiatives.**

- The State-level Committee on Nutrition Security, chaired by the Chief Minister, should facilitate the implementation of the numerous ongoing nutrition safety net programmes in a coordinated and mutually reinforcing manner in order to generate synergy and thereby maximise the benefits from the available resources.

- State governments should launch a nutrition literacy movement and set up "Media Coalitions for Nutrition Security" for improved nutrition awareness.

## 5. Action at national level: Mainstream nutrition in national missions.

- Appoint a Nutrition Advisory Board for large national programmes such as the Rashtriya Krishi Vikas Yojana, the National Horticulture Mission and the National Food Security Mission so that cropping and farming systems are anchored on the principle of food-based nutrition security.
- Organise the delivery of various nutrition safety net programmes on a lifecycle basis so that integrated attention can be given to the needs of an individual from birth to death.
- Open nutrition clinics and a PDS (Public Distribution System), outlet at the NREGS (National Rural Employment Guarantee), sites.
- Add a nutrition component to the NRHM (National Rural Health Mission), and thereby launch an Integrated National Rural Health and Nutrition Mission.

India has the resources to deal with the problem. It also has the knowledge and the expertise. Most of the solutions are well known. What then explains the slow progress? Clearly, it is insufficient State action.

There are at least three reasons. First, the government needs to "walk the talk". Despite identifying under-nutrition as a national shame, nutrition has not been assigned top priority and necessary resources have not been committed. Two, there is a reluctance to restructure, and if necessary dismantle and redesign, the ICDS programme despite several proposals for making it more efficient and effective. Three, there is a strong resistance to reorganise service delivery in order to ensure delivery of nutrition programmes for children.

☆☆☆☆☆

# 11 CHAPTER

# CHILD PARTICIPATION – KEY TO EFFECTIVE DEMOCRACY

**"A nation is democratic to the extent that its citizens are involved, particularly at the community level. The confidence and competence to be involved must be gradually acquired through practice ... there should be gradually increasing opportunities for children to participate in any aspiring democracy ..."** —*Roger Hart.*

Though the literature on child rights has increased in recent times, awareness and understanding of the concept is still limited. Three reasons help to explain this:

1. Children's rights have not generally been acknowledged as part of a 'sub set' of 'human rights'. Human rights groups have in the past felt that their work would be taken less seriously if child rights are explicitly recognized as part of 'human rights'.
2. In virtually all societies there is a strong bias against the idea of children as individuals in their own right making their own social, economic and cultural contribution. It is especially the case with girls.
3. Children's needs are viewed as synonymous with the needs of their families. Child rights are accepted as adults' responsibilities (generally parents or guardians and the state) so far as they relate to survival, development and protection.

The rights of children to participate in matters that affect their lives is least well understood. Children's rights to participate in decisions that affect their lives are generally treated by adults with either non-comprehension or ridicule! A frequent assertion about child participation is "How can children decide what is right or wrong? They are not mature enough!" This is based on certain assumptions about levels of participation and about children.

## DEFINITION

**'Participation' means children and young people**

- thinking for themselves
- expressing their views effectively
- interacting in a positive way with other people.

'Participation' means the involvement of girls and boys in the decisions and actions that affect their lives, the lives of their families and community and the larger society in which they live.

## WHY IS PARTICIPATION IMPORTANT?

The arguments for participation by children in development activities can be briefly summarised as:

**From efficiency** – it is more productive (in terms of use of resources and drawing on local knowledge systems) for children to participate in matters that affect them rather than be excluded.

**From enrichment** – by participating in matters that affect their lives children, can contribute to and enhance the quality of decisions taken and thereby gain useful insights.

**From empowerment** – by participating in decisions that affect them, children's capacities and capabilities can be developed and they gain more control over decisions that shape their lives.

The argument from efficiency can be broadly equated with economics, the argument from enrichment is generally used in cross-cultural discourse, whereas the argument from empowerment can be broadly equated with *political* (not *party political*) processes. The empowerment approach seeks to develop skills, knowledge and experience amongst the participants themselves. Participation by children in decisions that affect their lives can similarly be justified on the grounds of efficiency, enrichment or empowerment depending on the specific circumstances.

A typical Indian parent would be alarmed about the idea of involving their children in "political processes". It is however important to note that this process is part of a wider socialisation and growing-up process that children in all societies undergo.

**Three key points to note here are:**

i. The degree of opportunity for a child to collaborate in the everyday management of family, schools, neighbourhood and community groups is a reflection of the participatory opportunities available for adults in that culture.

ii. Children's participation does not mean supplanting adults. Adults do, however, need to learn to listen, support and guide; and to know when and when not to speak.

iii. Through their participation in activities children can be more "visible" in development planning and policy making.

According to the 1991 census in India the number of people under the age of 16 comprised almost 36% of the total population. For development agencies to exclude such a large segment of the population from participating in decision making (by focusing only on adult participation) is therefore an act of grave folly. Just as the importance of participation by women in decision making has been acknowledged, in a similar way children's involvement and participation in development also needs to be promoted. By doing this one can effectively contribute to a deepening and widening of democracy.

In most poor households (especially in poorer countries), children often contribute to the well being of other household members. There is sufficient evidence to suggest that children's productive contribution to household well being has been grossly underestimated. The universal tendency in families is not to recognise the capacities of children as decisionmakers even when, as workers, they are critical to the economy of the family.

If adult participation in politics aims to promote democracy and enable responsible citizenship, participation by children in decisions that affect their lives can lay the foundation for this process. There is an inherent contradiction in excluding children from participation in decisions that affect their lives and yet expecting adults (at the age of 18) to actively and responsibly participate in decision making. Hence it is possible to build a basis for democracy, and responsible and capable citizens for the future, by enabling children to participate in decisions that affect their lives.

## LEVELS OR LADDERS OF PARTICIPATION

Children are not seen as a separate or lesser category of person. They evolve into adulthood with the passage of time, gain experiences, assume responsibilities and go on to the next stage. It legitimises the arguments about increasing levels of participation - for adults as well as for children.

Roger Hart presents a 'beginning typology' for analysing children's participation in development projects which is in the form of a 'ladder of participation'.

1. **Manipulation** is the lowest rung on the ladder. Here the adults have complete and unchallenged authority and abuse their authority by failing to use it in the best interests of the children.

2. **Decoration** is the second rung of the ladder. An example might be when a group of children are asked to sing a song about rights for an audience of adults attending an international conference on children's rights.

3. **Tokenism** is used to describe when children are apparently given a voice, but in fact have little or no choice about the subject or the style of communicating it, and little or no opportunity to formulate their own opinions. A child's attendance as a speaker at a predominantly adult event might be an example unless the following requirements are met.

- The children must understand the purpose of the activity.
- They must know who made the decisions concerning their involvement and why.
- They should have a meaningful role.
- They should volunteer for the activity after the activity was made clear to them.

4. **Assigned but informed** means that the children are asked to volunteer for an activity when the above conditions are met. It is the first rung on the ladder of genuine participation.

5. **Consulted and informed** describes the situation where children's opinions are given genuine weight when they are consulted by adults. It is increasingly built in to child care legislation though it rarely leads to young people having significant influence over the use of resources.

This degree of participation is often found in the private sector where children's views may be sought in 'product testing' of consumer goods and services which are targeted specifically at them.

6. **Adult-initiated, shared decisions with children** is the first 'rung' of effective participation. Although the services, projects or activities are still initiated by adults, children are genuinely involved in the decisionmaking which shapes the way these are planned, carried out and evaluated.

7. **Child initiated and directed** activities are those where children establish their own priorities independently of adults. This happens most often in play but the approach can be used in the design and management of services. Genuine direction by children requires control over the allocation and use of resources.

8. **Child-initiated, shared decisions with adults** means that the initiative comes from the children, and adults may be required to mobilise resources or act as a facilitator but not to 'lead'. The outcome of the children's activity may well be communicated to adults who may be asked to act on their decisions to bring about some change desired by the children (for example, by altering agency policies or priorities or by providing new types of services requested by the children). This is an example of a partnership which could be applied even to the provision of statutory services where the adults are the agents of State service provision for children but may have some control over the nature of these services.

A variation is proposed by Barbara Franklin (1995). Her modified ladder begins with several rungs in which there is no participation and children are ignored, in the middle stages there are various degrees of consultation, and at the top of the ladder there are projects characterised by child initiated and directed actions in which "children are in charge".

**These typologies suggest that:**

a. Participation is not an end in itself. The opportunities for children's to participate in decisions that affect their lives largely reflect the participatory opportunities available for adults in a particular culture or community.

b. Children's participation does not mean supplanting adults. Adults need to learn to listen, support, facilitate and guide.

c. Genuine involvement fosters motivation.

d. Even when participation is encouraged it does not necessarily lead to children having a genuine role in decision making.

e. There are different levels of participation which can be broadly classified.

The ability to truly participate depends on a basic competence of an individual to understand the perspective of other persons. In a limited way children can generally do this by the age of three, but the process of being able to simultaneously identify with another perspective, while maintaining one's own view, continues to develop through adolescence. Research in the West suggests that the process of "perspective -taking ability" begins in the second or third year of a child's life. Up to the age of 5 or 6, although children become more aware that others around them have feelings, there is still confusion between the subjective psychological, and the objective or physical characteristics of a person's behaviour. Hence, intentional and unintentional behaviours of others are not differentiated. Gradually the "perspective-taking ability" improves so that between 5 and 9 years of age children become capable of clearly differentiating the physical and psychological characteristics of a person. During this period, most children realise that each person has their own unique, subjective view of the world.

Between the ages of 7 and 12, children begin to be able to step outside their own perceptions, to reflect on their interactions with others, and realise that other people can do the same thing. This phase of "sequential perspective-taking ability" means that two children now realise that they can put themselves "in each others shoes". They also recognise that people may have multiple or mixed feelings, such as being interested and happy, but a little frightened.

In the next stage, between 10 to 15 years, "mutual perspective-taking ability" children develop the ability to organise themselves into "enduring democratic groups". Young people spontaneously coordinate their perspectives with those of others. Beyond this, lies a stage where people begin to comprehend "multiple mutual perspectives forming a generalised societal, legal, or moral perspective in which all individuals can share". This "final stage" can emerge at any time after the age of 12 and that this stage enables the most fruitful cooperation between children.

**One might conclude that:**

1. Children do participate to a lesser or greater extent in decisions that affect their lives. This needs to be recognised.
2. If we aim to understand children and childhoods more, we must involve children in this process rather than interpret their lives through adult perceptions.
3. Children's participation can be viewed as part of a "political process" if it seeks to develop their capacities, capabilities and learning, and enables them to gain more control over decisions that affect their lives. Children's participation can also be promoted for other reasons including efficiency and enrichment.
4. Children are not a homogeneous group. They have different aspirations, needs and agendas.
5. The ability of children to participate depends on a variety of factors including competence to understand the perspective of other persons. It is important that advocates of child participation take into account age, class, gender, culture, (dis)ability and other factors which may shape the ability of an individual child to participate in a development project.

## WAYS OF PARTICIPATION

**Children and young people can participate (as individuals or as organised groups) by:**

- speaking out -**examples,** expose abuse, make a complaint about services, ask questions, raise awareness of a problem, press for a change in policy
- being involved in decisionmaking - **examples,** assessing needs, designing projects/programmes, sharing in school management, drawing up policy guidelines, developing legislation, evaluating services
- practical action - **examples,** peer education, setting up a child-led initiative or child-led organisation, carrying out research, children's involvement in the media.

**Adults, including parents teachers and development workers, play an important role in supporting children's participation. They can do this through:**

- encouraging children's involvement
- sharing information
- modelling participatory behaviour
- developing the skills needed for participation
- creating safe environments for children to practise participation.

## IMPORTANCE OF CHILD PARTICIPATION

**1. It is a child's right – examples,**

- participation is an essential characteristic of the child as an active subject of rights;
- it is seen as a general principle of fundamental importance to implementation of all aspects of the Convention on the Rights of the Child.

**2. It increases the effectiveness of interventions aimed at improving children's lives – examples,**

- it allows children to contribute to the analysis of how particular decisions or actions will serve their best interests;
- it ensures that projects, programmes and services are more appropriate, relevant and sustainable;
- it provides new perspectives on issues that are relevant to children (child labour, the impact of HIV/AIDS);
- it helps to identify the key barriers that children face in securing their rights and innovative responses to address them;

- it gives children more ownership and sense of responsibility for projects and services developed for their benefit;
- it leads to better decisions that build on children's own experience and knowledge.

**3. It brings benefits to the children involved – examples,**

- direct improvements in their own lives and life chances (access to schooling);
- the possibility to protect themselves and challenge abuses of rights;
- enhanced self-confidence and self-esteem; an opportunity to acquire and expand their skills;
- familiarisation with group and democratic processes;
- a sense of purpose and competence on their own lives and on the lives of their peers, families and community;
- an opportunity to learn and practise the skills of responsible and active citizenship.

**4. It empowers children as members of civil society and as active, responsible citizens – examples,**

- they can exercise their responsibilities and strengthen their ability to hold others (organisations, governments, institutions) to account;
- it allows them to play an active part in civil society and compensates for their relative exclusion from formal political processes;
- it increases the visibility of children and children's issues and places them on economic, social and political agendas;
- it increases adults' understanding and appreciation of children's capacities and is part of a process of changing attitudes towards children;
- it increases accountability to children (by enlarging the democratic space and encouraging good governance).

**5. Girls and boys themselves want to participate.**

**The Principles of Meaningful Participation**

Meaningful children's participation is characterised by:

- An ethical approach and a commitment to transparency, honesty and accountability (impact on decisionmaking).
- A safe approach in which children's protection rights are safeguarded.
- A non-discriminatory approach that ensures that all children (regardless of their class, gender, ability, language, ethnicity, sexual preference, religion, etc.) have an equal opportunity to be involved.

- A 'child-friendly' approach which enables children to contribute to the best of their abilities (good information, availability of venues, procedures and support that encourage rather than hinder children's involvement).

## KEY COMPONENTS OF MEANINGFUL PARTICIPATION OF CHILDREN (PRINCIPLES AND METHODS)

### Information and communication

- Ensure the issue is well-understood (using verbal and non-verbal means).
- Start from scratch and raise awareness with children so that they find their voice.
- Avoid jargon, make sure children's understanding of issues is clear and also of adults.
- Challenge is for adults to really listen to what children are saying.
- Begin the process at their level.
- Children should be consulted on their own terms.

### Environment and processes necessary for child participation

- Build trust so child is comfortable, part of whole process, and can opt out.
- Protection is key, information is confidential.
- Process is non-discriminatory.
- Ensure that children realise and feel strongly that their input is going to be taken seriously in final outcomes and they will be involved in full process, including follow up.
- Non-discrimination is an issue.
- Include children who are not perceived as being discriminated against.
- Bring children really together.
- Open avenues for children according to their evolving capacities.
- Create a safe environment so that children feel free to speak without threat or fear.
- Choice to participate or not. Be clear that it is their right to participate.

### Involving adults

- Involvement of whole family.
- Two way process – prepare the adults as well.
- Adequate preparation of both adults and children.
- Context of culture and behaviour – sensitive to context of children and community in which they live, includes preparation of adults for this cultural context.

### Keeping it relevant

- Intervention should address the context of the children involved.
- Diversity of response – children are not a homogenous group.

### Follow-up

- Responsibility for immediate task in hand as well as follow up with children and adults involved (learning for life process).
- Sustainability and ownership of any process involving children.

### Ethical issues (these pervade all of the above too)

- Safe environment and the ethical issue of what happens when children leave the safe environment that has been created for them.
- Be clear what are the criteria and principles for ethical and meaningful participation.
- What do we do when children say things we do not like? This is linked to ethical issues, representing views of all children.
- Ethical and other issues needing to be addressed for meaningful participation

## ETHICAL ISSUES RELATING TO CHILDREN PARTICIPATION

Establishing safe and meaningful environments for the participation of children, which minimise the risk to them from their involvement, does not happen by accident. The right environment needs to be created by ensuring:

*An ethical approach – **examples,***

- countering the imbalance in power and status between adults and children;
- ensuring children are able to freely express their views and opinions, that they are listened to seriously and that their views and opinions are taken into account;
- being clear about the purpose of participation (both adults and children) – what it involves and what impact it might have;
- providing children with access to relevant information about their involvement;
- giving children time to consider their involvement and give their personal informed consent to it;
- sensitising the adults involved in working with children and being responsive to the context in which the children live

*That children's participation is relevant and voluntary – **examples,***

- children have the choice whether to participate or not;

- children participate on their own terms and for lengths of time chosen by them;
- children are involved in ways, at levels and at a pace appropriate to their capacities and interests;
- child-centred ways of working are used and methods of involvement incorporate and build on supportive local structures and knowledge

*A 'child-friendly' enabling environment* – ***examples,***

- child-centred ways of working to build the confidence and self-esteem of children;
- time and resources are made available for quality participation;
- child-friendly spaces are identified and created where children feel comfortable;
- accessible information is shared with children in good time, in child-friendly formats and in languages that they understand

*That participation promotes the safety and protection of children* – ***examples,***

- everything is done to minimise the risk to children of abuse and exploitation or other negative consequences of their participation;
- ensuring the confidentiality and anonymity of children and respecting their boundaries (right of disclosure chosen and decided by children);
- ensuring that children's participation in the study does not increase their exposure to violence;
- ensuring that the necessary support is available if children's participation risks them reliving the trauma of violence

*That the selection of child participants or representatives is based on principles of democracy and non-discrimination* – ***examples,***

- children are involved in setting the criteria for selection and representation;
- that children should be able to select from among their peers those who will represent them in any of the study's initiatives

*Follow-up and evaluation* – ***examples,***

- committing from the beginning of the process to provide feedback and to follow-up and evaluate together with the children the quality and impact of their participation;
- make child-friendly versions of reports available in local languages so that children can access the outcomes of the study and their participation in it.

**The following considerations help in developing child-centred programmes and intervention:**

- Putting children at the centre, recognising them as rightholders and social actors..
- Recognising governments as primary duty-bearers accountable to their citizens' including children, and to the international community.

- Recognising parents and families as primary care-givers, protectors and guides and supporting them in these roles.
- Giving priority to children and to creating a child-friendly environment.
- Being gender and diversity sensitive and seeking inclusive solutions that involve a focus on those boys and girls who are at risk and who are discriminated against.
- Addressing unequal power structures (class, sex, ethnicity, age, caste, religion etc.).
- Holding a holistic vision of the rights of the child while making strategic choices and taking specific actions.
- Setting goals in terms of the fulfilment of rights.
- Aiming for sustainable results for children by focusing not only on the immediate, but also on the root cause of problems.
  - Using participatory and empowering approaches, in particular with regard to children.
  - Building partnerships and alliances for promotion of child rights.

☆☆☆☆☆

# 12 CHAPTER
# CHILD PROTECTION

**"All children behave as well as they are treated".** — *Jan Hunt*

India is home to almost 19% of the world's children. More than one third of the country's population, around 440 million, is below 18 years. India's children are India's future, as strength of the nation lies in a healthy, protected, educated and well-developed child population that will grow up to be productive citizens of the country. India must invest resources in children proportionate to their huge numbers.

The child internationally is defined as any person aged up to 18 years. In India, official convention has appeared to limit the definition to any person up to the age of 14 years (below 15 years). However, with the adoption of the Juvenile Justice Act (1986, amended in 2000), the National Plan of Action for Children 2005, and the Commissions for the Protection of Children's Rights Act 2005, the Government of India has now recognized that childhood legally extends to the age of 18 years.

ALL children have the right to be protected wherever they are – at home, in school, on the streets – and at all times, be they of peace or conflict or calamity. Their right to protection is as intrinsic to their well-being as is the right to survival, development and participation. Children deserve to live in an environment where good governance and the full enjoyment of human rights are mutually reinforcing.

## MEANING OF CHILD PROTECTION

In its simplest form, child protection addresses every child's right not to be subjected to harm. It thus complements other provisions that ensure that children receive all that they need in order to survive, develop and thrive.

Protection – from or against perceived or real risk, danger or damage – relates not only to a person's physical condition, but to all the nuances of life and status in diversity of physical, social, material, civil, cultural, psychological and political settings, and usually to a complex mix of them. In the case of children, it also relates to the child's capacity for self-reliance and self-defence as also to the role and responsibility of family, community, society and state.

*The Right to Protection:—* According to the CRC, this right includes freedom from all forms of exploitation, abuse and inhuman or degrading treatment. This includes the right to special protection in situations of emergency and armed conflict. The aim is simple, to protect vulnerable children from those who would take advantage of them and to safeguard their minds and bodies.

'Child Protection' is about protecting children from or against any perceived or real danger or risk to their life, their personhood and childhood. It is about reducing their vulnerability to any kind of harm and protecting them in harmful situations. It is about ensuring that no child falls out of the social security and safety net and, those who do, receive necessary care, protection and support so as to bring them back into the safety net. While protection is a right of every child, some children are more vulnerable than others and need special attention. The Government recognizes these children as 'children in difficult circumstances', characterized by their specific social, economic and geo-political situations. In addition to providing a safe environment for these children, it is imperative to ensure that all other children also remain protected. Child protection is integrally linked to every other right of the child. Failure to ensure children's right to protection adversely affects all other rights of the child. Thus, the Millennium Development Goals (MDGs) cannot be achieved unless child protection is an integral part of programmes, strategies and plans for their achievement. Failure to protect children from issues such as violence in schools, child labour, harmful traditional practices, child marriage, child abuse, the absence of parental care and commercial sexual exploitation among others, means failure in fulfilling both the Constitutional and International commitments towards children.

Both state and society are thus challenged to assure the child a protective environment and a caring community. In defining such an environment, UNICEF sets out eight elements which reflect the range of protective provisions the state should feel obliged to offer.

The child is entitled to protection against:

- The inequities of poor and stratified development services which impose unjust or inadequate conditions and standards of health, nutrition, education and what is meant to be care;
- Being rebuffed or ignored by substandard providers of services;
- Being denied a listing on official records, a name and a nationality;
- Being deprived of the enjoyment of his/her own culture, religion, language;
- Being stigmatized or marginalized because of his/her own culture, religion, language;
- Being targeted for discrimination or exclusion because of gender, caste, class or community, or due to a health or psycho-social condition;
- Being portrayed in a demeaning, derogatory or pornographic manner;

The Constitution of India recognizes the vulnerable position of children and their right to protection. Article 15 the Constitution guarantees special attention to children through necessary and special laws and policies that safeguard their rights. The Right to equality, protection of life and personal liberty and the right against exploitation is enshrined in Articles 14, 15, 16,

17, 21, 23 and 24.The child rights and welfare concerns have been addressed in a number of International Conventions and Standards on child protection including the UN Convention of the Rights of the Child (UNCRC) 1989, the UN Standard Minimum Rules for the Administration of Juvenile Justice (The Beijing Rules), 1985, the UN Rules for the Protection of Juveniles Deprived of their Liberty, 1990, and the Hague Convention on Inter-country Adoption, 1993. The Government of India ratified the UN Convention on the Rights of the Child (UNCRC) in 1992. The Convention prescribes standards to be adhered to by all State parties in securing the best interest of the child. It emphasises social reintegration of child victims, without resorting to judicial proceedings. The UNCRC outlines the fundamental rights of children, including the right to be protected from economic exploitation and harmful work, from all forms of sexual exploitation and abuse, and from physical or mental violence, as well as ensuring that children will not be separated from their family against their will.

India has adopted a number of laws and formulated a range of policies to ensure children's protection and improvement in their situation including, the Guardian and Wards Act 1890, Factories Act 1948, Hindu Adoption and Maintenance Act 1956, Probation of Offenders Act 1958, Bombay Prevention of Begging Act 1959, Orphanages and Other Charitable Homes (Supervision and Control) Act 1960, National Policy for Children 1974, Bonded Labour System (Abolition) Act 1976, Child Marriage and Restraint Act 1979, Immoral Traffic Prevention Act 1986, Child Labour (Prohibition and Regulation) Act 1986, National Policy on Education 1986, Prevention of Illicit Traffic in Narcotic Drugs and Psychotropic Substances Act 1987, National Policy on Child Labour1987, Infant Milk Substitutes, Feeding Bottles and Infant Foods (Regulation of Production, Supply and Distribution) Act 1992, National Nutrition Policy 1993, Pre-natal Diagnostic Techniques (Regulation and Prevention of Misuse) Act 1994, Persons with Disabilities (Equal Protection of Rights and Full Participation) Act 2000, Juvenile Justice (Care and Protection of Children) Act 2000, National Health Policy 2002, National Charter for Children 2004, National Plan of Action for Children 2005 and Commissions for Protection of the Rights of the Child, 2005.

However, these laws and policies promising respect for child rights, their protection and well being have not resulted in much improvement in lives of millions of Indian children who continue to be deprived of their rights, abused, exploited and taken away from their families and communities. Scant attention and feeble commitment to resolving child protection problems have resulted in poor implementation of these laws and policies; meagre resources; minimal infrastructure; inadequate services in variety, quantity and quality; and inadequate monitoring and evaluation. In light of its expanded mandate, the new Ministry of Women and Child Development views Child Protection as an essential component of the country's strategy to place '*Development of the child at the centre of the 11th Plan*'. Violations of the child's right to protection, in addition to being human rights violations, are massive, under-recognized and under-reported obstacles to child survival and development. Failure to protect children has serious consequences for the physical, mental, emotional and social development of the child, with consequences of a loss in productivity and quality of human capital for the nation.

The National Plan of Action for Children 2005 articulates the rights agenda for the development of children. The NPAC 2005 is the basis for planning for children in the Eleventh

Plan in all sectors and the principles articulated in it should guide the planning and investments for children. Such a comprehensive approach to child protection is required if India is to achieve Millennium Development Goals.

## EXISTING CHILD PROTECTION MECHANISMS IN INDIA

The existing institutions and programs for child protection in India primarily stem from the provisions under the Juvenile Justice (Care and Protection of Children) Act, 2000 and National Plan of Action for Children 2005. These comprise several programmes and schemes implemented by different ministries and departments among which are:

(i) **A Programme for Juvenile Justice** for children in need of care and protection and children in conflict with law. The Government of India provides financial assistance to the State Governments/UT Administrations for establishment and maintenance of various homes, salary of staff, food, clothing, etc., for children in need of care and protection and juveniles in conflict with law. Financial assistance is based on proposals submitted by States on a 50:50 cost sharing basis.

(ii) **An Integrated Programme for Street Children** without homes and family ties. Under the scheme NGOs are supported to run 24 hours shelters and provide food, clothing, shelter, non formal education, recreation, counselling, guidance and referral services for children. The other components of the scheme include enrolment in schools, vocational training, occupational placement, mobilizing preventive health services and reducing the incidents of drug and substance abuse, HIV/AIDS, etc.

(iii) **Childline Service** for children in distress, especially children in need of care and protection so as to rescue them from abuse, provide shelter to them, medical services, counselling, repatriation and rehabilitation.

(iv) **Scheme for Assistance to Homes for Children (Shishu Greha) to Promote In-Country Adoption** for care and protection of orphans/abandoned/destitute infants or children up to 6 years and promote their in-country adoption.

(v) **Scheme for Working Children in Need of Care and Protection** for children kept as domestic child labour, working at roadside dhabas, mechanic shops, etc. The scheme provides for bridge education and vocational training, medicine, food, recreation/sports equipment, etc.

(vi) **Rajiv Gandhi National Creche Scheme for the Children of Working Mothers** in the age group of 0-6 years. The scheme provides for comprehensive day-care services including facilities like food, shelter, medical, recreation, etc.

(vii) **Pilot Project to Combat the Trafficking of Women and Children for Commercial Sexual Exploitation** at source and destination areas for providing care and protection to trafficked and sexually abused women and children. Components of the scheme include networking with law enforcement agencies, rescue operation, temporary shelter for the victims, repatriation to hometown and legal services, etc.

**(viii) Central Adoption Resource Agency (CARA)** is an Autonomous Body under the Ministry of Women and Child Development to promote in-country adoption and regulate inter-country adoption. CARA also helps both Indian and foreign agencies involved in adoption of Indian children to function within a regulated framework, so that such children are adopted legally through recognised agencies and no exploitation takes place.

**(ix) National Child Labour Project (NCLP)** for rehabilitation of child labourers. Under the scheme, Project Societies at the district level are fully funded for opening up of Special Schools/ Rehabilitation Centres for the rehabilitation of child labourers. These special schools/rehabilitation centres provide non-formal education, vocational training, supplementary nutrition, stipends, etc., to children withdrawn from employment.

**State Governments Schemes:** Various State Governments are also running different state-specific schemes for institutional (residential) and non-institutional (non-residential) care of children in difficult circumstances.

## GLARING GAPS IN SERVICES

A close examination by the newly created Ministry of Women and Child Development of existing child protection schemes has revealed major shortcomings and gaps in existing child protection institutions, policies programs and their implementation at all levels. The minimal government structure that exists is rigid and a lot of time and energy are spent on maintaining the structure itself rather than concentrating on programmatic outcomes.

Existing programmes and schemes are marked by limitations such as:

**1. Lack of prevention**

Policies, programmes and structures to prevent children from falling into difficult circumstances are mostly lacking. This pertains both to policies to strengthen and empower poor and vulnerable families to cope with economic and social hardship and challenges and thus be able to take care of their children, as well as to efforts to raise awareness of all India's people on child rights and child protection situation.

**2. Poor planning and coordination**

(i) Poor implementation of existing laws and legislations;

(ii) Lack of linkages with essential lateral services for children, for example, education, health, police, judiciary, services for the disabled, etc.;

(iii) No mapping has been done of the children in need of care and protection or of the services available for them at the district/city/state levels;

(iv) Lack of coordination and convergence of programmes/services;

(v) Weak supervision, monitoring and evaluation of the juvenile justice system.

**3. Services are negligible relative to the needs**

(i) Most of the children in need of care and protection, as well as their families do not get any support and services;

(ii) Resources for child protection are meagre and their utilisation is extremely uneven across India;

(iii) Inadequate outreach and funding of existing programmes results in marginal coverage even of children in extremely difficult situations;

(iv) Ongoing large scale rural-urban migration creates an enormous variety and number of problems related to social dislocation, severe lack of shelter and rampant poverty, most of which are not addressed at all;

(v) Lack of services addressing the issues like child marriage, female foeticide, discrimination against the girl child, etc.

(vi) Little interventions for children affected by HIV/AIDS, drug abuse, militancy, disasters (both man-made and natural), abused and exploited children and children of vulnerable groups like commercial sex workers, prisoners, migrant population and other socially vulnerable groups, etc.

(vii) Little interventions for children with special needs, particularly mentally challenged children.

**4. Poor infrastructure**

(i) Structures mandated by legislation are often inadequate;

(ii) Lack of institutional infrastructure to deal with child protection;

(iii) Inadequate number of Child Welfare Committees {CWCs} and Juvenile Justice Boards { JJBs};

(iv) Existing CWCs and JJBs not provided with requisite facilities for their efficient functioning, resulting in delayed enquiries and disposal of cases.

**5. Inadequate human resources**

(i) Inappropriate appointments to key child protection services leading to inefficient and non-responsive services;

(ii) Lack of training and capacity building of personnel working in the child protection system;

(iii) Inadequate sensitisation and capacity building of allied systems including police, judiciary, health care professions, etc.;

(iv) Lack of proactive involvement of the voluntary sectors in child protection service delivery by the State/UT Administrations;

(v) Large number of vacancies in existing child protection institutions.

**6. Serious service gaps**

(i) Improper use of institution in contravention to government guidelines;

(ii) Lack of support services to families at risk, making children vulnerable;

(iii) Overbearing focus on institutional (residential care) with non-institutional (i.e. non-residential) services neglected;

(iv) Inter-state and Intra-state transfer of children especially for their restoration to families not provided for in the existing schemes.

(v) Lack of standards of care (accommodation, sanitation, leisure, food, etc.) in all institutions due to lower funding;

(vi) Lack of supervision and commitment to implement and monitor standards of care in institutions;

(vii) Most 24-hour shelters do not provide all the basic facilities required, especially availability of shelter, food and mainstream education;

(viii) Not all programmes address issues of drug abuse, HIV/AIDS and sexual abuse related vulnerabilities of children;

(ix) None of the existing schemes address the needs of child beggars or children used for begging;

(x) Minimal use of non-institutional care options like adoption, foster care and sponsorship, etc., to children without home and family ties;

(xi) No mechanism for child protection at community level or involvement of communities and local bodies in programmes and services;

(xii) Serious service and infrastructure gaps leading to few adoptions;

(xiii) Cumbersome and time consuming adoption services;

(xiv) Lack of rehabilitation services for older children not adopted through the regular adoption process;

(xv) Aftercare and rehabilitation programme for children above 18 years are not available in all States, and where they do exist they are run as any other institutions under the JJ Act 2000.

(xvi) Majority of services are of poor or extremely poor quality.

**7. Weak accountability, monitoring and evaluation**

(i) Reporting mechanism and accountability are not clearly defined and are rarely enforced in most of the programmes and schemes;

(ii) Monitoring mechanisms are not in place;

(iii) Data required for planning, policy making and monitoring is not available.

(iv) Evaluation is rarely done.

☆☆☆☆☆

13

CHAPTER

# THE INTEGRATED CHILD PROTECTION SCHEME (ICPS)

**"The best way to make children good is to make them happy." — *Oscar Wilde***

## PURPOSE

The Integrated Child Protection Scheme is expected to significantly contribute to the realization of Government/State responsibility for creating a system that will efficiently and effectively protect children. It is based on cardinal principles of "protection of child rights" and "best interest of the child". Hence, the ICPS objectives are: to contribute to the improvements in the well being of children in difficult circumstances, as well as to the reduction of vulnerabilities to situations and actions that lead to abuse, neglect, exploitation, abandonment and separation of children. These will be achieved by:

(i) improved access to and quality of child protection services;

(ii) raised public awareness about the reality of child rights, situation and protection in India;

(iii) clearly articulated responsibilities and enforced accountability for child protection

(iv) established and functioning structures at all government levels for delivery of statutory and support services to children in difficult circumstances;

(v) introduced and operational evidence based monitoring and evaluation.

## SPECIFIC OBJECTIVES OF ICPS

1. To institutionalize essential services and strengthen structures:

   (i) Establish and strengthen a continuum of services for emergency outreach, institutional care, family and community based care, counselling and support services;

   (ii) Put in place and strengthen necessary structures and mechanisms for effective implementation of the scheme at the national, regional, state and district levels;

   (iii) Define and set standards of all services including operational manuals for the functioning of statutory bodies.

2. To enhance capacities at all levels:

   (i) Build capacities of all functionaries including, administrators and service providers, at all levels working under the ICPS;

   (ii) Sensitize and train members of allied systems including, local bodies, police, judiciary and other concerned departments of State Governments to undertake responsibilities under the ICPS.

3 To create database and knowledge base for child protection services:

   (i) Create mechanisms for a child protection data management system including MIS and child tracking system in the country for effective implementation and monitoring of child protection services;

   (ii) Undertake research and documentation.

4 To strengthen child protection at family and community level:

   (i) Build capacities of families and community to strengthen care, protection and response to children;

   (ii) Create and promote preventive measures to protect children from situations of vulnerability, risk and abuse.

5 To ensure appropriate inter-sectoral response at all levels:

   Coordinate and network with all allied systems, i.e., Government departments and Non-Government agencies providing services for children for effective implementation of the scheme.

6 To raise public awareness:

   (i) Educate public on child rights and protection;

   (ii) Raise public awareness at all levels on situation and vulnerabilities of children and families;

   (iii) Inform the public on available child protection services, schemes and structures at all levels.

## GUIDING PRINCIPLES OF ICPS

1 **Child protection, a primary responsibility of family, supported by community, government and civil society.** It is important that respective roles are articulated clearly and understood by all parties in the effort to protect children. Government, both Central and State, has an obligation to ensure a range and a continuum of services at all levels.

2 **Loving and caring family, the best place for the child:** Children are best cared for by their own families and have a right to family care and parenting by both parents.

3 **Privacy and Confidentiality:** Children's right to privacy and confidentiality should be protected through all the stages of service delivery.

4 **Non-stigmatization and non-discrimination:** Each child irrespective of circumstances, as well as socio-economic, cultural, religious and ethnic background should be treated equally and in a dignified manner.

5 **Prevention and reduction of vulnerabilities, central to child protection outcomes:** A major thrust of the ICPS will be to strengthen the family capabilities to care for and protect the child.

6 **Institutionalization of children, the last resort:** There is a need to shift the focus of interventions from an over reliance on institutionalization of children and move towards more family and community–based alternatives for care. Institutionalization should be used as a measure of last resort after all other options have been explored.

7 **Child centered planning and implementation** : Planning and implementation of child protection policies and service delivery should be child centered at all levels, so as to ensure that the best interest of the child is protected.

8 **Technical excellence, code of conduct:** Services for children at all levels and by all providers should be provided by skilled and professional staff, including a cadre of social workers, psychologists, care givers, members of statutory bodies and lawyers, adhering to an ethical and professional code of conduct.

9 **Flexible programming, responding to local individualised needs:** Customized service delivery approach is required to respond to local needs.

10 **Good governance, accountability and responsibility:** An efficient and effective child protection system requires transparent management and decision making, accountable and responsible individuals and institutions, performance reports at all service levels and all service providers made public, including for children themselves, through child-friendly reports.

## APPROACHES OF ICPS

1 **Prevention:** Through an outreach programme, the scheme would identify and support vulnerable families. Trained district level functionaries through effective networking and linkages with the Village and Block Level Child Protection Committees, ICDS functionaries, NGOs and local bodies would ensure convergence of services. Community capacities for protection and monitoring shall be strengthened and child protection concerns and safeguards shall be integrated in all sectors.

2 **Promotion of Family-based Care:** The scheme would pursue a conscious shift to family-based care including sponsorship, kinship care, foster care and adoption. Periodic review of children in institutional care for restoration to families would also be undertaken.

3 **Financing:** As a centrally sponsored scheme financial assistance from the Central Government will be disbursed to the State Government/UT Administration. The Central Government shall provide a predetermined percentage of the budgeted cost. The State/UT shall in turn provide grant-in-aid to voluntary organizations under the different components of the scheme.

4 **Integrated service provision - range of services:** Through an interface with various sectors, including health, education, judiciary, police, and labour, among others, the scheme would strive to integrate service provisions into a range of services to cater to the multiple needs of children in difficult circumstances.

5 **Continuum of services — a feasible care plan for each child:** The services under the scheme will be provided on the basis of an individual care plan, established through professional assessment. The care plan must be periodically reviewed and accordingly adjusted. Adequate services should be available as long as the child is in need of care, including follow up.

6 **Community based service delivery:** The scheme would endeavour to bring services closer to vulnerable children and families for increased access. Child care services should be available at community level integrated into a range of services with strong linkages to the PRIs and local government bodies.

7 **Decentralization and flexibility to focus on local needs:** The scheme shall decentralize planning and implementation of child protection services at the State and District level based on specific needs. The allocation of human resource shall be based on protection service requirement for quality child protection services.

8 **Partnership Building and Community Empowerment:** A key strategy for programme development and implementation would be developing close working relationships, information sharing and strategy building between government structures, civil society organizations including corporate and communities.

9 **Quality care, standards for care and protection:** All protection services — be it public or privately provided — should adhere to prescribed standards pertaining to physical infrastructure and human resource requirements, as well as protocols, methodological instructions and guidelines for services and operational manuals for functioning of statutory bodies.

10 **Building Capacities:** In order to ensure professional child protection services at all levels, the scheme would undertake regular training and capacity building of all service providers and functionaries to equip and enhance their skills, sensitivities, knowledge on child rights and standards of care and protection.

## Target Groups

The ICPS will focus its activities on children in need of care and protection and children in conflict and contact with the law:

(a) **Child in need of care and protection** means a child who:

(i) is found without any home or settled place or abode and without any ostensible means of subsistence;

(ii) resides with a person (whether a guardian of the child or not) and such person has threatened to kill or injure the child and there is a reasonable likelihood of the threat being carried out, or has killed, abused or neglected some other child or children and there is a reasonable likelihood of the child in question being killed, abused or neglected by that person;

(iii) is a mentally or physically challenged or ill child or a child suffering from terminal diseases or incurable diseases, and/or having no one to support or look after him/her;

(iv) has a parent or guardian and such parent or guardian is unfit or incapacitated to care for or supervise the child;

(v) does not have a parent/parents and no one is willing to take care of him/her, or whose parents have abandoned him/her or who is a missing and/or runaway child and whose parents cannot be found after reasonable inquiry;

(vi) is being or is likely to be grossly abused, tortured or exploited for the purpose of sexual abuse or illegal acts;

(vii) is found vulnerable and is likely to be inducted into drug abuse or trafficking;

(viii) is being or is likely to be abused for unconscionable gains;

(ix) is victim of any armed conflict, civil commotion or natural calamity.

**(b) Child in conflict with law** is one who is alleged to have committed an offence.

**(c) Child in contact with law** is one who has come in contact with the law either as victim or as a witness or due to any other circumstancs.

The ICPS will also provide preventive, statutory and care and rehabilitation services to **any other vulnerable child including, but not limited, to:** children of potentially vulnerable families and families at risk, children of socially excluded groups like migrant families, families living in extreme poverty, scheduled castes, scheduled tribes and other backward classes, families subjected to or affected by discrimination, minorities, children infected and/or affected by HIV/AIDS, orphans, child drug abusers, children of substance abusers, child beggars, trafficked or sexually exploited children, children of prisoners, and street working children

## ICPS PROGRAMMES AND ACTIVITIES

Through ICPS, the Ministry of Women and Child Development envisages to carve out a broad and comprehensive framework for child protection in the Eleventh Plan and to set the foundation for creating a strong protective environment for children. Every child of India has the right to be cared for by a loving and nurturing family, to live with dignity, and to be protected from separation from her family, violence, abuse, neglect and exploitation.

The Integrated Child Protection Scheme will focus on:

(i) Mapping needs and services for children and families at risk;

(ii) Preparing child protection plans at district and state levels; the plan would be gradually extended to block and community levels;

(iii) Strengthening service delivery mechanisms and programmes including preventive, statutory, care and rehabilitation services;

(iv) Improving access to and quality of services provided;

(v) Promoting and strengthening non-institutional family- based care options for children deprived of parental care, including sponsorship to vulnerable families, kinship-care, in-country adoption, foster care and inter-country adoption, in order of preference;

(vi) Developing capacity of service providers;

(vii) Strengthening knowledge base, awareness and advocacy;

(viii) Establishing an integrated, live, web based data base (on children in difficult circumstances, children in care, service providers and services provided), for evidence-based monitoring and evaluation and service planning decision making;

(ix) Monitoring and evaluation;

(x) Building partnerships and alliances for child protection at all levels, particularly at the grassroot community and district levels.

(xi) Strengthening linkages with other bodies and institutions such as the National/State Human Rights Commissions and National/State Commissions for Protection of Rights of the Child, etc.

ICPS brings several existing child protection programmes under one umbrella and initiates new interventions.

## I. CARE, SUPPORT AND REHABILITATION SERVICES

### 1. Emergency outreach service through '*CHILDLINE*'

***CHILDLINE*** is a 24/7 emergency phone outreach service for children in need of care and protection linking them to emergency and long- term care and rehabilitation services. The service can be accessed by a child in difficulty or an adult on his behalf by dialing **1098**. Established by the Government of India in 1999, it is presently operational in 83 cities across the country. In order to create a protective environment for children in all parts of the country, ICPS envisages the expansion of the CHILDLINE service to all districts/cities.

### 2. Open shelters for children in need in urban and semi-urban areas

The large numbers of homeless children, pavement dwellers, street and working children and child beggars, left on their own and in need of care and support, is an urban phenomena of great concern. 29% of India's population resides in urban areas, half of which live in conditions of extreme deprivation compounded by lack of shelter and access to basic services like sanitation, safe drinking water, education, health care, recreational facilities, etc. The urban population is also expanding rapidly because of intense rural-urban migration, swelling cities and towns, further compromising the ability of civic authorities to meet people's basic needs. A large proportion of the migrant population ends up residing in inhuman conditions in slums, squatter colonies, railway platforms, pavements, bus stops, tourist spots, etc. As a result, urban poverty and hunger are increasing. In this situation, children suffer the most. A vast majority of them, with or without parental support, end up at traffic intersections, railway stations, streets, sabzi mandi (vegetable market), etc. They can be seen begging for alms, wiping automobile windscreens, rag picking, vending wares and may also be involved in petty thefts, drug peddling or controlled by a begging or stealing mafia. Many of these children also peddle sex for survival and paedophilia is common. These children are very often victims of adult abuse of all kinds: physical, sexual, emotional as well as economic exploitation. Inhuman and violent life conditions turn many of these children into law offenders, criminals, drug abusers and exploiters themselves. If continued to be neglected, not only are human lives and capital wasted, but such children also become a huge drain on society. Mainstreaming these children is a big challenge, compounded by the fact that they have no parental care and support. It becomes the responsibility of the State to meet their special needs. The State must create a flexible mechanism, which will meet the unique needs of these children, harness their talent and potential, thus giving them the opportunity to become productive citizens. In order to provide for the growing needs of these children, the ICPS would facilitate setting up open shelters particularly in urban areas. Such centres shall provide a space for children where they can play, use their time productively and engage themselves in creative activities through music, dance, drama, yoga and meditation, computers, indoor and outdoor games, etc. These activities would encourage meaningful peer group participation and interaction. This will ensure their overall growth and development, and keep them away from socially deviant behaviours in addition to fulfilling their basic requirements for food, nutrition and health. These shelters shall also have provisions for health care, quality and flexi-time education and vocational training, including provisions where children can safely keep their belongings and earnings. Counselling guidance and life skill education shall also be provided for channelling these children's energy into productive endeavours.

The objective of such a service is to provide an opportunity for the increasing number of vulnerable children in urban areas to be protected from abuse and neglect on the street and provide them access to alternatives. In the long term, these children would be weaned away from street life and enabled to lead a dignified and productive life.

**3. Family-based non-institutional care through Sponsorship, Foster-care, Adoption and Aftercare**

The Juvenile Justice (Care and Protection of Children) Act, 2000 and its Amendment Act, 2006 provides for the rehabilitation and reintegration of children through sponsorship, foster-care, adoption and after-care.

**i. Sponsorship**

Many children are at risk of abandonment, exploitation, neglect and destitution because of poor socio-economic conditions of their families. Poor families often place their children into institutional care as a poverty coping measure. In many other cases children run away from their families because of abuse and/or exploitative conditions and often do not want to be reunited with their families. Hence, they are placed in institutions. As a result, large numbers of children are forced to spend their lives in institutions. It is an accepted fact that institutionalisation of children should be the last resort and the family-based non-institutional care is a better option.

The Government of India realizes the importance of reintegrating, to the extent possible, institutionalized children into families. To that end, individual cases of children in institutions will be periodically reviewed and the reintegration into their biological family facilitated with necessary support and supervised financial assistance. Apart from the above categories of children, a significant number live in extreme conditions of deprivation or exploitation, with families who are unable to provide basic care and services to them. The Government of India also realizes the need to provide support and supervised financial assistance to such extreme cases as a preventive measure to keep children within families and remain protected. In order to achieve the above, the Government of India proposes a pilot initiative under the ICPS to provide support services to families at risk. ICPS shall create a special Sponsorship and Foster Care Fund within the DCPS. Sponsorship will offer supplementary financial support to families to meet the educational, medical, nutritional and other needs of children with a view to improving the quality of their lives.

**ii. Foster Care**

Fostering is an arrangement whereby a child lives, usually on a temporary basis, with an extended or unrelated family member. Such an arrangement ensures that the birth parents do not lose any of their parental rights or responsibilities. This arrangement shall cater to children who are not legally free for adoption, and whose parents are unable to care for them due to illness, death, desertion by one parent or any other crisis. The aim is to eventually re-unite the child with his/her own family when the family circumstances improve, and thus prevent institutionalization of children in difficult circumstances.

The scheme shall provide support for foster care through the Sponsorship and Foster Care Fund available with the District Child Protection Society. The Child Welfare Committee either by itself or with the help of SAA, shall identify suitable cases and order placement of the child in foster-care. Once the Child Welfare Committee orders the placement of the child in foster care, a copy of the order shall be marked to the DCPS for release of funds and to SAA for follow up and monitoring. The SAA shall periodically report about the progress of the child to the Child Welfare Committee and DCPS.

**iii. Adoption**

Adoption is a process through which a child who is permanently separated from biological parents because her/his parents have died, or have abandoned or surrendered her/him, becomes a legitimate child of a new set of parent(s) referred to as adoptive parents with all the rights, privileges and responsibilities that are attached to this relationship.

Central Adoption Resource Agency (CARA) is the nodal agency for coordinating the work and has been primarily engaged in streamlining inter-country adoption. The number of adoptions appears to have plateaued in the last five years necessitating a proactive intervention by the Ministry. ICPS therefore incorporates a series of steps aimed at streamlining the adoption process; addressing identified bottlenecks and regional disparities; and promoting national adoptions.

The adoption programme will be governed by the following guiding principles:

(i) Best interest of the child is paramount.

(ii) Institutionalization (e.g., placement into residential care) of the child should be for the shortest possible period of time

(iii) All attempts should be made to find a suitable Indian family within the district, state or country.

(iv) The child shall be offered for inter-country adoption only after all possibilities for national adoption, or other forms of family based placement alternatives such as placement with relatives (kinship care), sponsorship and foster care arrangements have been exhausted.

(v) All institutions should disclose details about children in their care and make sure that those free for adoption are filed and recorded with the State Adoption Resource Agency (SARA) and CARA, with all supporting documentation of authorization of such adoption from CWC.

(vi) Inter-state coordination to match the list of Prospective Adoptive Parents (PAPs) with that of available children should be done by SARAs.

(vii) No birth mother/parent(s) should be forced/coerced to give up their child for monetary or any other consideration.

(viii) Adoption process from the beginning to end shall be completed in the shortest possible time.

(ix) Monitoring, regulating and promoting the concept and practice of ethical adoptions in the country should be ensured.

(x) Agencies involved in the adoption process should perform their duties in a transparentmanner, following rules of good governance and adhering to the professional and ethical code of conduct. Those agencies shall be reporting to and will be subject to rigorous auditing and supervision by responsible State bodies.

The Inter-country adoption in India shall be guided by the Hague Convention on Inter-Country Adoption - 1993, signed by India on 9th January, 2003 and ratified on 6th June, 2003. Following the best interest of the child, the convention gives priority to in-country adoption, while inter-country adoption is considered only as the last care.

**iv. Cradle Baby Reception Centre**

At least 60 million girls who would otherwise be expected to be alive are "missing" from various populations, mostly in Asia, as a result of sex-selective abortions, infanticide or neglect. In India too female foeticide is a cause of growing concern, especially in states like Punjab, Haryana, Delhi, Himachal Pradesh and Gujarat, where the girls to boys ratio has "drastically declined": to fewer than 800 girls for every 1,000 boys. In India as a whole, this ratio has declined from 945 girls per 1,000 boys aged 0-6 in 1991 to 927/1,000 in 2001, indicating the seriousness of the problem. Recognizing the fact that over 80% of districts in the country do not have facilities to receive or offer temporary shelter for children in crisis situation, especially those who are abandoned and vulnerable to be trafficked, the ICPS envisages setting up Cradle Baby Reception Centres in each district. These Cradle Baby Reception Centres will be linked to Cradle Points at Primary Health Care Centres (PHCs), Hospitals/Nursing Homes, Swadhar Units, Short Stay Homes and in the office of the DCPS to receive abandoned babies. For every child received by the cradle baby reception centre, the process of creating an individual care plan shall be initiated by the reception centre, to be further developed and prepared by the SAA in whose care the child is to be transferred after the authorization of the CWC.

**v. After-care Programme**

The Juvenile Justice (Care and Protection of Children) Act, 2000 provides for institutional care for juveniles in conflict with law and children in need of care and protection up to the age of 18 years. However, most of the children in care have nowhere to go once they reach the age of 18 and are discharged from their institutions. In addition, as empirically observed, institutional life does not prepare children well for life outside an institution. They are unable to sustain themselves and are easily affected by negative influences. There is a need to prepare these children to sustain themselves during the transition from institutional to independent life. The District Child Protection Society shall be responsible for developing an After-care programme. Based on the case to case basis, a JJB/CWC can order placement of a juvenile/child in the after-care programme.

### 4. Institutional Services

As provided by the Juvenile Justice (Care and Protection of Children) Act, 2000, the scheme shall support the creation of new institutional facilities and maintenance of existing institutional facilities for both children in conflict with law and children in need of care and protection. For each child in institutional care, an individual care plan shall be developed by the concerned agency in consultation with the DCPS within a month.

### 5. Shelter Homes

While a large number of urban marginalized children are in need of day care services, there are many others who require residential care for a temporary period for one or more reasons. These include children without parental care, runaway children, migrant children, etc. The Juvenile Justice (Care and Protection of Children) Act, 2000 empowers State Governments to recognize reputed and competent voluntary organizations, who cater to the needs of such children. The State Government shall provide financial assistance to set up and administer Shelter Homes for such children. These Shelter Homes shall offer day and night shelter facilities to the children in need of support services for a temporary period, while efforts are made to rehabilitate them. In order to facilitate and expedite the setting up of Shelter Homes in every district or group of districts, the scheme shall provide financial support to the State Governments and Union Territories.

### 6. Children's Homes

A large number of children in need of care and protection who enter the juvenile justice system through the Child Welfare Committees (CWCs) are in need of residential care and protection during the pendency of any inquiry and subsequently for their long-term care, treatment, education, training, development and rehabilitation. The Juvenile Justice (Care and Protection of Children) Act 2000 empowers the State Government either by itself or in collaboration with voluntary organizations to set up Children's Homes in every district or group of districts for the reception and residential care of such children. These homes shall serve as a home away from home and provide comprehensive child care facilities to children for ensuring their all-round development. They shall work towards enhancing the capabilities and skills of children and work with their families with the view of facilitating their reintegration and rehabilitation into mainstream society.

### 7. Observation Homes

Children in conflict with law who enter the juvenile justice system through the Juvenile Justice Boards (JJBs) are in need of adequate residential care and protection during the pendency of any inquiry regarding them under the Juvenile Justice (Care and Protection of Children) Act 2000. The Act empowers the State Governments to establish and maintain either by itself or under an agreement with voluntary organizations, observation homes in every district or group of districts for their temporary reception. In order to facilitate and expedite setting up of Observation Homes in every district or group of districts, the scheme shall provide financial support to the State Governments and Union Territory Administrations.

### 8. Special Homes

Children in rehabilitation and protection require institutional services. The State Governments are empowered to establish and maintain either by itself or under an agreement with voluntary organisations, special homes in every district or group of districts for the reception and rehabilitation of juveniles in conflict with law.

In order to facilitate and expedite setting up of Special Homes in every district or group of districts, the scheme shall provide financial support to the State Governments and Union Territory Administrations.

### 9. Specialised Services for Children with Special Needs

A significant number of children affected by HIV and AIDS and substance abuse, as well as mentally or physically challenged children are in need of long term care because of abandonment, death of one or both parents or inability of parents to care for them. Such children are especially vulnerable as they are least likely to have family care alternatives and hence, require specialized institutional care and treatment including medical, nutritional, and psychological support. The growing epidemic of HIV and AIDS in India has affected the lives of children in many ways. Infected children (those who are HIV+) are often in need of long term special care to fight the disease. Many affected children those who either live with a family member suffering from AIDS, or have lost their parents and/or other family members to AIDS, need assistance and support because of their family circumstances. Similarly, there is a large number of children in difficult circumstances in India, because of substance abuse, including children who are either drug addicts themselves or are affected because their parents or other family members are drug addicts. Some children are used by drug traffickers as carriers of drugs and they often slowly fall into the trap of substance abuse, often leading to delinquent behaviour. It has also been observed that poverty and lack of social security and medical services tend to cause parents to abandon children with physical and mental disability. Such children are also in need of specialized care and services to meet their health, nutrition, educational, etc., needs and emotional well-being. The scheme shall provide an additional component to institutions having children with special needs and shall provide flexibility to the State Government to either integrate the programme for children with special needs in its existing institutions or support setting up of specialized homes for such children.

## II. STATUTORY SUPPORT SERVICES

### 1. Child Welfare Committees (CWCs):

The Juvenile Justice (Care and Protection of Children) Amendment Act, 2006 recently passed by both houses of Parliament makes it mandatory to establish one Child Welfare Committee in each district as the final authority to dispose of cases for the care, protection, treatment, development and rehabilitation of children in need of care and protection and to provide for their basic needs and protection of human rights.

To facilitate the setting up of CWCs in every district and to ensure their effective functioning, the scheme shall provide adequate infrastructure and financial support to the State Governments and UT Administrations.

### 2. Juvenile Justice Boards (JJBs):

The Juvenile Justice (Care and Protection of Children) Amendment Act, 2006 makes it mandatory to have one Juvenile Justice Board in each district to deal with matters relating to juveniles in conflict with law. To facilitate setting up of a JJB in each district and to ensure their effective functioning, the scheme shall provide adequate infrastructure and financial support to State Governments and UT Administrations.

### 3. Special Juvenile Police Units (SJPUs):

The Juvenile Justice Act, 2000 provides for setting up Special Juvenile Police Units in every district and city to coordinate and upgrade the police interface with children. All the police officers, designated as juvenile/child welfare officers in the district or city, are members of the SJPU. As a statutory requirement, the ICPS shall provide for two paid social workers in each SJPU for supporting the unit. The District Child Protection Society shall appoint these social workers and depute their services to the SJPU as and when necessary. Of the two Social Workers, at least one should be a woman and another having expertise in child protection.

## III. OTHER ACTIVITIES

**1. Human resource development for strengthening counselling services:**

Counselling for children and families at risk is an integral component of the ICPS. Acknowledging the lack of such a cadre, the ICPS envisages development of a cadre of counsellors to provide professional counselling services under various components of the scheme. National Institute of Public Cooperation and Child Development (NIPCCD) and its four regional centres shall initiate professional counselling courses, by themselves and through the aegis of schools of social work, departments of social science, etc. Such courses shall be accredited through a relevant institution/body.

**2. Training and capacity building:**

There is an acute shortage of professionally trained manpower to provide comprehensive services to children in difficult circumstances. Training is required for (a) new recruits under the ICPS; (b) existing manpower that need capacity enhancement and sensitization. Training and capacity building of all personnel involved in the child protection sector throughout the country including those working under the ICPS shall be taken up on priority basis. Such personnel need to be trained and groomed to join the child protection workforce to provide child friendly services at all levels.

**3. Strengthening the knowledge-base:**

The creation of a protective environment for children requires strong knowledge base of information for developing informed and strategic responses. Lack of data adversely affects planning, the provision of appropriate services and allocation of resources. Under the ICPS following specific measures shall be developed and strengthened:

**i. Research and documentation:** In order to develop effective intervention strategies and implement child protection programmes to reach every child, there is a strong need for availability of comprehensive information base and documentation of best practices. The scheme would facilitate carrying out comprehensive studies to assess the causes, nature and extent of specific child protection issues like trafficking and commercial sexual exploitation of children; violence against children; children in conflict with the law, child marriage, infanticide/foeticide, children in urban situations and any other area.

The scheme would also support research in areas of potential or new threats to child protection to build knowledge, evidence and integrate the learning into policies and programmes. These would include issues related to livelihood and security, migration, internal displacement, child abuse and exploitation, child pornography and other emerging issues and their relationship to child rights.

**ii. Child Tracking System:** The Ministry of Women and Child Development recognizes that at present there is acute shortage of data and information pertaining to issues related to child protection. Due to this gap, there is no comprehension about the dimension of the problem, i.e., number of children requiring support and the kind of services they are in need of. In order to bridge this gap, the Ministry of WCD, under the ICPS, will develop an effective system for child protection data management and reporting as well as a tool for monitoring the plementation of all its child protection schemes. This is to be achieved by developing a web-enabled data anagement system on child protection by creating a resource base for child protection issues. It is also planned to develop a nationwide website for tracking missing children and their ultimate repatriation and rehabilitation.

This is a complex and intensive activity demanding a lot of time and resources, and would therefore be gradually developed and expanded to the entire country. The Child Tracking System will be setup by the Central Project Support Unit (CPSU) under the ICPS. The CPSU will develop uniform data entry mechanisms and unified procedures for enabling centralized coordination through effective use of web-enabled software that will be developed for the purpose. At the State level SPSU and SCPS with support of DCPS will set up and manage this child tracking system.

**4. Monitoring**

Monitoring shall be carried out at district, state and national levels. At each level, a standardized format and a minimum set of input, output and outcome indicators for evidence based monitoring shall be established. Monitoring system shall be supported by an automated management information system. The information collected through the assessment of institutions set up under the Juvenile Justice (Care and Protection of Children) Act, 2000 and its Amendment Act, 2006 across the country would serve as the baseline for developing this management information system. Initially, the DCPS shall collect, upgrade and maintain disaggregated database manually and would initiate such efforts within one month of being established. The State level database shall be maintained at SCPS on the basis of inputs from the DCPSs. The district and state-wise database would gradually be developed into a web enabled management information system on child protection by the end of Eleventh Plan.

**i. Monitoring at District level:** The Chairperson Zila Parishad and District Magistrate, assisted by District Child Protection Committee (DCPC), shall supervise the activities of the DCPS as well as the overall implementation of the ICPS. Such a Committee under the Chairpersonship and Co-chairpersonship of the Chairperson Zila Parishad and District Magistrate respectively shall include members from the allied government departments like health, education, labour, housing, judiciary, home, railways; members of local bodies like PRIs, ULBs; and members of voluntary organizations and civil society. The DCPC shall monitor the implementation of ICPS on the basis of district-specific indicators, which will be developed in the process of implementation of the scheme.

**ii. Monitoring at State level:** The State Secretary, Women and Child Development shall supervise the implementation of ICPS with the help of the State Child Protection Committee (SCPC). Such a Committee under the Chairpersonship of the State Secretary shall include members from the allied government departments like health, education, labour, housing, judiciary, home, railways and members of the local bodies like PRIs, ULBs, voluntary organizations and members of the civil society. The SCPC shall monitor the implementation of ICPS on the basis of the state specific indicators, which will be developed in the process of implementation of the scheme. The Chief Secretary of the concerned State/UT shall conduct an annual review and evaluation of the implementation of the ICPS at State level. The Ministry of Women and Child Development shall develop set of guidelines for annual review of the implementation of the scheme on the basis of which the annual review will be carried out and report sent to the Government of India.

**iii. Monitoring at Central level:** The Ministry of Women and Child Development shall monitor and supervise the implementation of the ICPS at national level by:

(a) Holding an annual review meeting of State Secretaries;

(b) Closely monitoring the level of implementation in the States by holding quarterly review meetings in the States;

(c) Providing technical support for effective implementation of the scheme;

(d) Instituting national level awards to encourage excellence in service delivery.

**5. Evaluation**

Since ICPS is a new scheme and will be implemented in a phased manner, a mid-term evaluation of the scheme shall be conducted at the end of the second year of the implementation to evaluate effectiveness and suggest course correction. This will be followed by a final evaluation at the end of the Eleventh Five Year Plan. The Ministry of Women and Child Development will have these evaluations conducted by an independent agency.

☆☆☆☆☆

# 14 CHAPTER

# CHILD FRIENDLY SCHOOL

**"Even minimal amounts of spanking can lead to an increased likelihood in antisocial behavior by children".** —***Andrew Grogan-Kaylor.***

UNICEF has developed a framework for rights-based, child-friendly educational systems and schools that are characterized as "inclusive, healthy and protective for all children, effective with children, and involved with families and communities and children" (Shaeffer, 1999). Within this framework:

- The school is a significant personal and social environment in the lives of its students. A child-friendly school ensures every child an environment that is physically safe, emotionally secure and psychologically enabling.
- Teachers are the single most important factor in creating an effective and inclusive classroom.
- Children are natural learners, but this capacity to learn can be undermined and sometimes destroyed. A child-friendly school recognizes, encourages and supports children's growing capacities as learners by providing a school culture, teaching behaviours and curriculum content that are focused on learning and the learner.
- The ability of a school to be and to call itself child-friendly is directly linked to the support, participation and collaboration it receives from families.
- Child-friendly schools aim to develop a learning environment in which children are motivated and able to learn. Staff members are friendly and welcoming to children and attend to all their health and safety needs.

### A framework for rights-based, child-friendly schools

All social systems and agencies which affect children should be based on the principles of the Convention on the Rights of the Child. This is particularly true for schools which, despite disparities in access across much of the world, serve a large percentage of children of primary school age.

Such rights-based — or child-friendly — schools must not only help children realize their right to a basic education of good quality but also need to do many other things like—help children learn what they need to learn to face the challenges of the new century; enhance their health and well-being; guarantee them safe and protective spaces for learning, free from violence and abuse; raise teacher morale and motivation; and mobilize community support for education.

## A RIGHTS-BASED, CHILD-FRIENDLY SCHOOL HAS TWO BASIC CHARACTERISTICS

- **It is a child-seeking school** — actively identifying excluded children to get them enrolled in school and included in learning, treating children as subjects with rights and State as duty-bearers with obligations to fulfill these rights, and demonstrating, promoting, and helping to monitor the rights and well-being of all children in the community.
- **It is a child-centered school** — acting in the best interests of the child, leading to the realisation of the child's full potential, and concerned both about the "whole" child (including her health, nutritional status, and well-being) and about what happens to children — in their families and communities - before they enter school and after they leave it.

Above all, a rights-based, child-friendly school must reflect an environment of good quality characterized by several essential aspects:

**It is inclusive of children — it:**

- Does not exclude, discriminate, or stereotype on the basis of difference.
- Provides education that is free and compulsory, affordable and accessible, especially to families and children at risk.
- Respects diversity and ensures equality of learning for all children (e.g., girls, working children, children of ethnic minorities and affected by HIV/AIDS, children with disabilities, victims of exploitation and violence).
- Responds to diversity by meeting the differing circumstances and needs of children (e.g., based on gender, social class, ethnicity, and ability level).

**It is effective for learning — it:**

- Promotes good quality teaching and learning processes with individualizd instruction appropriate to each child's developmental level, abilities, and learning style and with active, cooperative, and democratic learning methods.
- Provides structured content and good quality materials and resources.
- Enhances teacher capacity, morale, commitment, status, and income — and their own recognition of child rights.
- Promotes quality learning outcomes by defining and helping children learn what they need to learn and teaching them how to learn.

**It is healthy and protective of children — it:**

- Ensures a healthy, hygienic, and safe learning environment, with adequate water and sanitation facilities and healthy classrooms, healthy policies and practices (e.g., a school free of drugs, corporal punishment, and harassment), and the provision of health services such as nutritional supplementation and counseling.
- Provides life skills-based health education.
- Promotes both the physical and the psycho-socio-emotional health of teachers and learners.
- Helps to defend and protect all children from abuse and harm.
- Provides positive experiences for children.

**It is gender-sensitive — it:**

- Promotes gender equality in enrolment and achievement.
- Eliminates gender stereotypes.
- Guarantees girl-friendly facilities, curricula, textbooks and teaching-learning processes.
- Socializes girls and boys in a non-violent environment.
- Encourages respect for each others' rights, dignity, and equality.

**It is involved with children, families, and communities — it is:**

- Child-centred — promoting child participation in all aspects of school life.
- Family-focused — working to strengthen families as the child's primary caregivers and educators and helping children, parents, and teachers establish harmonious relationships.
- Community-based — encouraging local partnership in education, acting in the community for the sake of children, and working with other actors to ensure the fulfillment of childrens' rights.

Experience is now showing that a framework of rights-based, child-friendly schools can be a powerful tool for both helping to fulfil the rights of children and providing them an education of good quality. At the national level, for ministries, development agencies, and civil society organizations, the framework can be used as a normative goal for policies and programmes leading to child-friendly systems and environments, as a focus for collaborative programming leading to greater resource allocations for education, and as a component of staff training. At the community level, for school staff, parents, and other community members, the framework can serve as both a goal and a tool of quality improvement through localized self-assessment, planning, and management and as a means for mobilizing the community around education and child rights.

☆☆☆☆☆

# BIBLIOGRAPHY


Adams, E. and Ingham, S. (1998). Changing Places: Children's Participation in Environmental Planning. The Children's Society, London.

Advisory Group on Citizenship (1998). Education for Citizenship and the Teaching of Democracy in Schools.

Archard, D. (1993). *Children: Rights and Childhood*, London, Routledge.

Arnold, C. et., *al.*, (2000). Bringing up Children in a Changing World: Who's Right? Whose Rights? Conversations with Families. Save the Children and UNICEF.

Arnold, C. (2002). 'Are Younger Children Being Sidelined in the Child Rights Movement? The Importance of ECD Programmes to Ensuring Children's Rights. Monitor. Vol.15, p.13-18.

Bell, B. (1999). The Beginnings of a Journey: Making a Reality of Children's Citizenship. Bill Bell, Advocacy Unit, Save the Children UK. Paper delivered to a workshop held in Lima, Peru 18 May 1999.

Butler, I. and Williamson, H. (1994). *Children Speak: Children, Trauma and Social Work.* NSPCC/ Longman: Exeter.

Boyden, J. and Ennew, J. (eds.), (1997). *Children in Focus - A Manual for Participatory Research with Children.* Save the Children Sweden Publication.

Butterflies "Children's Organisation Balloon Poster", Delhi, India (contact: butterflies@vsnl.net.in).

Child-to-Child (1992). *A Resource Book. Part 1: Implementing the Child-to-Child Approach.* Child-to-Child Trust: London.

Clark, A. and Moss, P. (2001). Listening to Young Children: The Mosaic Approach, *National Children's Bureau, London.*

CRIN (2002). Children and Young People's Participation. *CRIN Newsletter.*

Cussianovich, A. (1995). 'Working Children and Adolescents: Culture, Image and Theory'. *NATs Working Children and Adolescents International Review,* 2/1995, 27-32.

Cohen, J. and Emanuel, J. (1998). *Positive Participation, Consulting with Children and Young*

*People in Health- related work: A Planning and Training Resource.* Health Education Authority, London.

Ennew, J. (1995). 'NATs (Working Children and Adolescents): Historical Emergence of a Category.' *NATs Working Children and Adolescents International Review,* 2/1995, 19-26.

Fajerman, L., Jarrett, M., Sutton, F. (2000). Children as Partners in Planning. Save the Children.

Fewkes, J. H., and Bhat, M. S. (2002). Our Voices.... Are you Listening? Children's Committee for Village Development. Save the Children UK, India.

Jones, H. (1999). *Including Disabled Children People in Everyday Life: A Practical Approach.* SCUK, London.

Johnson, V., et al. (Eds) (1999). *Stepping Forward: Children and Young People's Participation in the Development Process.* Intermediate Technology Publication.

Greig, A. and Taylor, J. (1999). *Doing Research with Children,* Sage Publications.

Hart, R. (1992). *Children's Participation: From Tokenism To Citizenship.* Florence: UNICEF.

Hart, R. (1997). *Children's Participation: The Theory and Practice of Involving Young People in Community Development and Environmental Care.* Earthscan, London.

Hurley, N. (1998). Straight Talk - Working with Children and Young People in Groups. Joseph Rowntree Foundation.

James, A. and Prout, A. (1990). *Constructing and Reconstructing Childhood: Contemporary Issues in the Sociological Study of Childhood (Eds).* The Falmer Press, London.

Kan, I. (2000). Children's Response to the Aral Sea Crisis. *Children, Citizenship and Environmental Conference.*

Karkara, R. and O'Kane, C. (2002). A new era of young citizens. CRIN Newsletter on Children and Young People's Participation.

Lansdown, G. (1995). *Taking Part: Children's Participation in Decision-Making.* IPPR: London.

Lansdown, G. (2001). *Promoting Children's Participation in Democratic Decision-Making.* UNICEF

Law, S. et al. (2001). Research Ethics. Save the Children UK, 2001.

Laws, S. (1998). Hear Me! Consulting with Young People on Mental Health Series, *Mental Health Foundation*, London.

Lewis, I. (2000). Accessibility and Participation. SC UK, London.

Lewis, A. and Lindsay, G. (2001). *Researching Children's Perspectives.* Open University Press.

Matthews, H., Children and Community Regeneration: Creating Better Neighbourhoods, Save the Children, London.

McCrum, S. (1998). Interviewing Children - A Guide for Journalists and Others. Booklet and Audio Tape.

McGuigan, C. (2003). Advocacy Impact Assessment: A Literature Review. Save the Children UK.

McNeish, D. (1999). From Rhetoric to Reality: Participatory Approaches to Health Promotion with Young People. *Health Education Authority*, UK.

Milner, P. and Caroline, B. eds. (1999). *Time to listen to children.* Routledge.

Morrow, V. and Richards, M. (1996). 'The Ethics of Social Research with Children: An Overview.' *Children and Society*, Vol.10, No.2, 90-105.

Miller, J. (1999). *A Journey of Discovery: Children's Creative Participation in Planning.* Save the Children.

Putti, J. (1993). *The Fair Deal: A Resource Book on Value Education in Social Justice*. Kristu Jyoti College, Bangalore, India.

My Name is Today: Special Focus: Participation, Vol. VIII, Nos. 1 & 2. Butterflies, New Delhi.

Nair, D. (1996). Child-Centred Participatory Research. Integrated Education for the Visually Impaired – Some Insights. SC UK.

O'Kane, C. (2002). 'Marginalised Children as Social Actors for Social Justice in South Asia', *British Journal of Social Work,* 32, p.697-710.

'O'Kane, C. and Sen, I. (2001) *'In Search of Fair Play: Street and Working Children Speak about Their Rights'*. Butterflies and Mosaic: India.

Ormidian, P. (Dr.) (2000). Impact of SC UK Child-Focused Health Education Project: Effects on Children's Self-Esteem and Status in the Family. SC UK, Afghanistan Office.

Oxfam (1985). *The Field Directors Handbook: An Oxfam Manual for Development Workers.* Edited by Brian Pratt and Jo Boyden. Oxford, University Press.

Panicker, R. and O'Kane, C. (2000). 'What Accounts for Success in Developing Children's Organisations' in Strategy Workshop Report on Children, Citizenship and Governance. Save the Children OSCAR, Nepal.

Petren, A. and Hammarberg, T. (2000). 'The Political Influence of Children'. In Children's Rights : Turning Principles into Practice. Save the Children and UNICEF.

Raman, V. (2000). Childhood - Western and Indian, An Exploratory Essay. *Centre for Women's Development Studies*: New Delhi.

Ranjani, R. Rajesh. August 2001. Working Papers Series: The Participation Rights of Adolescents: A Strategic Approach. New York: UNICEF.

Reddy, N. and Ratna, K. (2002). A Journey in Children's Participation. The Concerned for Working Children, India.

Reddy, N. (2000). Children As Partners In Change: Children, Citizenship And Governance). Unpublished Keynote Address in The Baspcan Congress, York, September 2000.

Save the Children (1995). *Towards a Children's Agenda: New challenges for social development. Save the Children UK*, London.

Save the Children (2001). *'We are Citizens'*. Save the Children South and Central Asia. A film made on a Regional Training Workshop on Children, Citizenship and Governance, December 2000, New Delhi.

Save the Children (2001). Theatre for Development Training Manual. Save the Children UK Office for South and Central Asia region.

Save the Children UK (2001). *Working Better with Children: Children Having a Greater Voice.* in Save the Children UK. Pilot CD Rom Resources, Save the Children UK.

Save the Children (2002). *'Training Tool for Facilitators on Child Participation'*. Southzone, Save the Children UK India.

Save the Children (2002). *A Summary Guide for Governments* to Support Children and Young People's Participation in National Plans of Action. (see www.savethechildren.net).

Save the Children (2002) *A Summary Guide for Civil Society* to Support Children and Young People's Participation in National Plans of Action. (see www.savethechildren.net).

Save the Children Alliance (2002). *Child Rights Programming: How to Apply Rights-Based Approaches in Programming: A Handbook for International Save the Children Alliance Members.*

Sutton, F. et., *al*. (1999). *The School Council: A Children's Guide.* Save the Children (Midlands Development Team).

Thomas, N., O'Kane, C., Phillipson, J. and Davies, E. (1998). *Children and Decision-Making Toolbox and Training Pack.* [The box includes a summary of the research, a 90-page training guide, pictorial and bilingual 'topic cards', a board game, 'Success', and the 'Voices with Volume' tape of children's words] Available from Children in Wales, Cardiff, Wales, UK.

Treseder, P. (1997). *Empowering Children and Young People: Training Manual.* Children's Rights Office/ Save the Children: London.

UNICEF (1997). *Education for Conflict Resolution: A Training for Trainers Manual.* UNICEF.

UNICEF (2002). State of World Children Focus on *Participation*. UNICEF.

UN Convention on the Rights (1997). *An International Save the Children Alliance Training Kit.*

Waitt, C. (1998). *Reaching Out: Consultation with 'Hard to Reach' Users of Mental Health Services.* Barnados.

Worrall, S. (2000). *Young People as Researchers, a Learning Resource Pack*. Save the Children UK and Joseph Rowntree Foundation.

Videos and CDs

Graue, M. and Walsh, D. (1998). Studying Children in Context. Theories, Methods and Ethics. Sage Publications.

Ward, L. (1997). Seen and Heard: Involving Disabled Children and Young People in Research and Development

Projects. Joseph Rowntree Foundation.

Watson, D. (Eds.) (1985). A Code of Ethics for Social Work: The Second Step. BASW and RKP.

Wellard, S. (Eds.) All Together Now. Community Participation for Children and Young People, SCUK.

White, S (2001). Child Brigade: An Organisation of Street Working Children in Bangladesh. Save the Children Sweden, Dhaka

Whittles, S. (1998). *Can You Hear Us? Including the Views of Disabled Children and Young People in Decision Making.* SC Publication.

Wilkinson, J. (2000). *Children and Participation - Research, Monitoring and Evaluation with Children and Young People.* Save the Children UK.

Williams, J. (2000). Think Country Child! The Councillors Guide to Planning Services for Children and Young People in Rural Areas. NCVCCO, CA, LGA, London.

Willow, C. (1997). *Hear! Hear! Promoting children and young people's democratic participation in local government.* Local Government Information Unit Woodhead, M. (1998).

Children's Perspectives on their Working Lives. A Participatory Study in Bangladesh, Ethiopia, The Philippines, Guatemala, El Salvador and Nicaragua. Radda Barnen.

Youniss, J., Silbereisen, R., Christmas-Best, V., Diversi, M., Bales, S., and McLaughlin, (2002). Youth Civic Engagement in the 21st Century. *Journal of Research on Adolescence*, volume 12, issue 1.